COME
GO
HOME
WITH
ME

COME GO HOME WITH ME

....

Stories by

SHEILA KAY ADAMS

Foreword by Lee Smith

The University of North Carolina Press

Chapel Hill and London

© 1995

The University of

North Carolina Press

All rights reserved

Manufactured in the

United States of America

The paper in this book

meets the guidelines for

permanence and durability

of the Committee on

Production Guidelines

for Book Longevity

of the Council on

Library Resources.

Library of Congress

Cataloging-in-Publication Data

Adams, Sheila Kay.

Come go home with me: stories / by Sheila

Kay Adams. Foreword by Lee Smith.

p.   cm.

ISBN 0-8078-2243-4 (cloth: alk. paper). —

ISBN 0-8078-4536-1 (pbk.: alk. paper)

1. Title.

PS3551.D395315B35   1995   95-8516

813'.54 — dc20   CIP

99   98   97   96   95   5   4   3   2   1

This book is lovingly

dedicated to my children,

Melanie Michelle Rice,

Hart Adams Barnhill,

and

Andrew Taylor Barnhill.

They are my reasons . . .

Contents

Foreword

Every time I hear Sheila Adams sing a ballad, a chill runs through my body like a brushfire, and the hair on my arms rises straight up. Sheila stands firm and tall to sing – feet apart, hands clasped, face lifted, eyes closed – and gives it everything she's got. Her dark hair falls down past her waist. She's not thinking about the audience, if there is one; she's not thinking about anything except the song. Each line ends in a little fillip – an abbreviated keening sound, a cut-off wail – that indicates the pathos that is the stuff of these songs. Her voice is full of power, wisdom, pain. Upon meeting her, most listeners have the same surprised reaction I did: you can't believe she's so young.

But Sheila comes by her authority honestly. She's a seventh-generation ballad singer, born and raised in the remote settlement of Sodom, way up in mountainous Madison County, North Carolina, which Bascom Lamar Lunsford once referred to as "the last stand of the natural people." When Cecil Sharpe was collecting ballads there in the early 1900s, he commented that Madison County was a place where people sang as easily as they talked. Sheila says, "I fell in love with the frailing banjo on first hearing it, but there was always something about the ballads that touched me deep inside, even back when I was knee-high to a grasshopper" – especially as sung by Granny, along with other Sodom singers like Berzilla Wallin, Cas Wallin, Vergie Wallin, and Inez Chandler.

"It ain't surprising," Granny told her. "It's 'cause it's yourn."

Sheila was learning to play the "old two-finger style" banjo from her uncle, Byard Ray, and her cousin, Jerry Adams. "Then when I was nineteen," she says, "these four men from West Virginia got a grant from the Rockefeller Foundation to come to Sodom and put on a festival. One of them, Dwight Diller, played clawhammer banjo. I just had to learn it."

Sheila has been singing professionally for years, though her "day job" until recently was teaching school in Madison County. She graduated from Mars Hill College in 1974. She has won many awards, including First Place Old Time Banjo at the 1991 Mountain Dance and Folk Festival. Recently she has added storytelling to her repertoire and has turned into a full-time performer.

I first ran into Sheila at a writing workshop that poet Kay Byer and I were conducting over in Cullowhee. The first exercise was simple: close your eyes, imagine a special place from your childhood, and write about it. On the spot, Sheila wrote the first draft of "It's a Sign," the first piece in this collection. As she read the story to us, we listened, transfixed. Two of the women were crying.

Sheila finished reading the story and looked up at us.

"I don't know how to write a story," she said.

"Oh yes you do," we assured her. *Oh yes. You do.* And now she has written a lot of stories. Some of them are the old tales handed down through her family; others are Sodom stories from the not-so-distant past; still others are Sheila's own as she grows up and goes away and comes to understand the value and uniqueness of her heritage. Though Sheila's granny, Dellie Chandler Norton, whom she calls "the most exciting person I have ever known and the best teacher I would ever have," sometimes threatens to run away with this book, finally it is Sheila's own story she's telling here, from a perspective of "years later and a woman grown."

And not only her own – for Sodom was (and *is*, for yet a little while longer) a *community*, a place where everybody knew everybody and who their people were.

And Sheila knows them all – you'll meet Bertha and the snake handlers; Little Corrie, who took a notion to change her husband's suit after he was already in his coffin; Chester, who is always trying to save Briar's soul; and

Sheila's own beloved grandfather, Breaddaddy, who taught her about death and dying with a graveyard dance.

By turns hilarious and deeply moving, always lively, Sheila's stories paint the portrait of a whole culture, from the past to the present day. Many outsiders have traveled into Appalachia for the purposes of "finding material" or cataloging this culture. Sheila *is* the material; she *is* the source.

Lee Smith
Jefferson, North Carolina
June 1994

Preface

• • • • • • • • • • • • • • • • • • • •

Folks in Sodom used to say, "Come go home with me." In the following stories, I am inviting you to do just that.

Sodom is a community located in the mountains of western North Carolina. The main valley forks off into three coves – the Ben Cove, the Burton Cove, and the Rice Cove. From the highest ridge tops you can see all the way to the Great Smokies of Tennessee. You also get a feeling of how closed in the community is as you look out at the mountains rolling and tumbling away off into the hazy blue folds that make up the Blue Ridge Mountain chain. It is a beautiful place, my Sodom.

Sodom got its name back during the Civil War. The story goes that there was a regiment of Confederate soldiers camped down around Hot Springs and a Union regiment camped right over the line in Tennessee. Right where Sodom is located, there resided a band of prostitutes that "serviced" both regiments. A circuit-riding Baptist preacher came through the area and held a revival. He commented from the pulpit that there was more sinning went on in that little community than went on in Sodom in the Bible. The War ended, the prostitutes moved on, but the name stuck.

As with most places, what made Sodom special was its people. The first settlers came there in the late 1700s. They were mostly Scots-Irish – fiercely independent, hard-working, hard-drinking, quick to anger and to fight folks. The reason they were called Scots-Irish is because they came here from Scotland by way of Northern Ireland, where they had moved and later had been persecuted by the English. They came full of hope for a better life, and they found it here in the mountains. They lived pretty much to themselves until the English and Germans came seeking a place to raise their families in peace. The English and Germans married into the families of the Scots-Irish, and now it's impossible to find a single person that doesn't claim roots with all three nationalities.

This book is a journey. Often during the trip I found myself homesick for the place and the people of my childhood. I recalled the beloved faces and familiar voices so clearly in my memory that I dreamed of them at night. I would wake with that childhood anticipation we all have experienced, only to realize that Sodom was gone. It existed only in the pages of this book. So, in a way, I hate to finish with these writings. By sharing them with you, maybe the people that populate my dreams can find a place in your heart, too.

This book is dedicated to my three children. It's only fitting. See, as I would put them in bed at night when they were small and lean down to kiss them good night, one or the other would say, "Mama, tell us a story about when you were a little girl growing up in Sodom." It had to be a different story every night. I really had to do some remembering. And then they began to ask for favorites. So the stories began to develop into what you will be reading. My daughter, Melanie, who is twenty-three now, says it was through these stories that she began to learn about herself. I agree. I feel as strongly now as I did back then – it is only through our past that we can prepare ourselves for the future.

So, thank you for coming. Welcome to Sodom.

COME
GO
HOME
WITH
ME

It's a Sign

There was a small branch that wound and twisted its way down from the Sim Top, through the Burton Cove, on down through Sodom, and later joined with Big Laurel Creek. It wasn't very wide or deep, but in places it formed pools that were so clear that you could see the sand and rocks on the bottom. It was the perfect place for minners to live. As children, we would make hooks out of straight pins, catch a few worms, and fish for those little fellers. We always put them right back in the water so there never got to be a shortage of them.

One hot September day, I was helping Granny clean up after breakfast. She brought the tail of her apron up and wiped the sweat off her face. "Hit's hotter 'an Satan's house cat today."

She walked to the open door and stood, one arm braced against the facing, and looked for all the world a picture, framed and motionless. Then she whirled of a sudden and said, "Grab a flour sack, honey. Let's go to the woods and gather us some buckeyes. We'll git us a dope from the peddler."

She reached around behind her and untied her apron and threw it over the back of one of the kitchen chairs. I reached in the kitchen cupboard and brought out a flour sack that bore the same pattern as the underwear I had on, and out into the sunshine we sailed, Granny in front, singing at the top of her lungs, me in tow. Granny's digging stick swung gracefully from the leather string around her neck, and she paused briefly to grab her hoe from where it leaned against the barn. She never went into the woods without her digging stick, the handle worn smooth from years of use digging out 'sang root. And she never went without her hoe, the edge of which was honed to razor sharpness. The hoe served a dual purpose. It could be used as a walking stick on the steep mountainsides, or it could slice the head off a copperhead in one blow. Granny was an accomplished copperhead killer.

By midafternoon, we had filled the flour sack full to busting, had located several 'sang roots, two of which were now in Granny's possession to be washed and hung behind the stove, where they would dry and later be sold. We had turned over rocks in the branch so we could watch the spring lizards jump straight up and then slither farther into the mud to be still as death, and we had a run-in with a huge thousand-legs. Granny capped her hand over my mouth when we saw the thousand-legs, because if you show them your teeth, they'll every one rot out.

We had wandered through the mountains and gradually worked our way back down to the branch, where we laid down on our stomachs and watched the minners dart back and forth through the shafts of sunlight that sifted down through the leaves of the buckeye trees. We dipped our fingers into the water and the minners came right up; and if we stayed real still, they would nibble our fingertips. If we moved our hands the slightest bit, they would streak off in all directions, only to return when the water became still again.

Suddenly, out of nowhere, came the sound of a strong breeze – but the air was perfectly still. Granny looked up and about that time a big yellow and black butterfly landed on the bank beside her, and then another, and another. They swooped down out of the sky and covered the banks of the stream, the trunks of the trees, and me and Granny. They settled on our arms, our hair, our faces. I will never forget the way Granny looked with her hair and face, arms, and shoulders all covered with butterflies opening and closing their wings. Granny's skin looked to be a moving, living mass of yellow! And through the living yellow I could see Granny's shining blue eyes. I got so excited that I jumped up and started trying to catch them, and Granny spoke sharply to me for one of the first times in my life.

"Git down an' be still, girl!"

I was so startled and hurt by Granny's tone of voice that I did as I was told immediately. The butterflies soon settled back on me, and I looked at those on my arm. I could see their tiny bright eyes, their curled velvet tongues; even more, I thought I could see their "life's-blood" running through their paper-thin wings.

And then, in a fluid and beautiful motion, they lifted as one and spiraled into the blue September sky and were gone. Granny reached out and took me in her arms and held me fiercely for a minute.

"It's a sign, Sealy, it's a sign of some kind. God sent them butterflies just for us. I'm sure it's a sign . . ."

Time passed; it always does. I still remember, though. And sometimes in the heat of late summer or early fall, I go back to the little branch there beneath the huge buckeye trees and sit on the bank with my feet dangling in the water, searching in vain for the minners that nibbled at my finger thirty years ago. And I turn my face up, searching the endless blue for a cloud of yellow, listening for the rustle of a thousand little wings.

Marking a Trail

Breaddaddy was my mother's father. His voice was a constant throughout my childhood, and I can hear it in my mind even today. He was a small man, "razor-blade thin," as he used to refer to himself, with a thick shock of stiff white hair and all of his "God-given teeth." He was a great source of entertainment for me as a child and one of the best storytellers I've ever heard.

Me and Breaddaddy used to hunt bird nests in the field there next to the house. We would crawl along on our bellies, him in front parting the tall grass, me close behind. I would look back every now and again, marveling at how the grass stayed flat. Breaddaddy said we were marking our trail.

"We'd be in trouble if they was somebody a trackin' us, Grandbaby. Why, that grass a layin' down that a way would lead 'em straight to us. You have to be clever when you don't want to be cotch up with."

We'd find a bird's nest, and, every time, he would caution me about not touching the nest or even allowing my breath to pass over it. "Iffen the Mammie bird even so much as gets one whiff of our smell on the babies, she'll leave the nest and the babies will die."

I believed him. I had seen the results before. The tiny defenseless babies tossed from the nest, flopping along on the hard ground, covered in ants. I knew better than to touch them.

One day, Breaddaddy decided to take me to the High Rock to pick blackberries. We left early, and midmorning found us sitting on the top of the ridge in the shade of the High Rock.

The High Rock was a strange jumble of rocks, some of them rising up into the air for thirty feet or more. The fact that they were right out on the top of the ridge always caused me to go into a full-blown question-asking fit.

"How did these rocks git here? Who was the first person to ever see them? Reckon they was left here by them big glaciers? How long do you reckon they've been here like this? And what about them holes up there in the rock? How do you reckon they got there?" And on and on. I guess it was in self-defense that Breaddaddy told me this story.

"A way back, years ago, even before your people come to Sodom, they was wild animals that roamed through here – big black bears that stood ten feet high when they rared up on their back legs, the big cats, them what was black, and the brown'uns too, prowled these woods. We had beaver that lived up and down the branches, and flyin' squirrels and wild turkey and even had wolves.

"The Indians farmed the land just like we do. They had crops a growin' right out the ridge there. They cleared and farmed the ridge tops first 'cause they caught the sun better and they could see clear out across the valley in case danger threatened. They was a clever bunch, the Indians. They lived close to the land and knew how to take care of it. They was real careful with it and it was good to them, too.

"They was a young Indian girl that used to come and help her Mam and Pap work. They would leave home before daylight and work all day out here on the ridge. She was a good girl, and part of her job was to help take care of her little brothers and sisters. See, they couldn't take the young'uns to the field and put 'em down on a quilt the way your Ma did when we went to the fields. They was always havin' to worry about some wild animal a carryin' them off and eatin' them. So, the young girl stood watch.

"Now, the young girl was really purty, and when she got up courtin' age, she drew the unwanted attention of one of the braves there in her village. He was a bad 'un and there was talk that he had taken his wife off and killed her. They never was able to prove it, so he was a free man. This man took to followin' the girl and her family up on the ridge and would set off to the side and watch the girl as she took care of the young'uns. She was afraid of him and tried not to even look at him as he set up on that rock over there. But she knew he was there.

"One mornin', as she sat with the young'uns, the brave got up from where he usually sat and walked over to the biggest rock, that one right over there, and started to chip away at the face of the rock. The girl watched, wonderin' what in the world he was doin'. He never said a word, just kept strikin' that rock, blow after blow. By the time the girl and her family left the ridge, he had a purty good sized hole started.

"This went on for weeks. He made seven perfectly round holes; count 'em, you'll see there's only seven."

I wandered over to the rock and climbed up on a fallen tree and peeked in the lowest of the seven holes. I rubbed my hand over the inside, feeling the smoothness of the rock. Breaddaddy's voice went on behind me.

"Well, he chiseled out them seven holes just as purty as you please and went back to settin' on his rock. Now, he had a mean face on him. Had a big scar that ripped down the right side of his cheek. He picked that up in a knife fight about the time his wife disappeared.

"The girl was afraid of him. Afore long though, her curiosity overcome her fear. She went over to the rock, right about where you are, and peeped in, just like you're a doin'. There was a real purty white deer hide neatly folded layin' inside.

"The girl took it out and felt the leather. She glanced over at the rock right nervous-like and the brave smiled and nodded at her. She carried the hide back over to where her brothers and sisters were a sittin' and kept her back turned to the brave the rest of the day.

"The next day, she wandered back over to the rock and climbed up and peeped in the second hole. They was a beautiful feather necklace a layin' there. She reached in and touched the feathers. She picked it up and lifted it out of the hole, turned, and looked at the brave, and he nodded and smiled with his scarred mouth. She looked longer this time, thinkin' how black his hair was with the sun hittin' it that way.

"The third day, she almost ran to the third hole in the rock. Hit was even higher and she had to stand up on a tree trunk, just like you're a doin'. They was one of the finest baskets a settin' there that the girl had ever seen. She took it out and turned to where the brave sat. She smiled at him, thinkin' how if he turned his scar away, he weren't near as ugly.

"Now, this went on for four more days. Each mornin' the young, beautiful girl would find somethin' just as grand as what she had found the mornin' before. By the seventh day she was a havin' a struggle reachin' the mouth of the hole. The seventh one was just too high for her. She tried ever' way she knew to get up to it. Finally, she looked over at the brave, and he smiled. She smiled back at him, and they stood lookin' at each other. He stood and walked over to where she was. He made a stirrup out of his two hands and offered it to her. She stepped up into his hands and he lifted her up to the seventh and final hole in the rock. See it up there? That's the one.

"Well, she reached in and pulled out a beautiful, carved cradle board. Now, the young girl knew what this meant, and she looked down into that ugly, scarred face and smiled.

"They married. And they had seven children, and folks say that the meanness went right out of him. Whenever they come up here to work the fields, they would put their young'uns in them holes so the wild animals couldn't get at them.

"When the soldiers come to take them away in the 1830s, they didn't want to go. See, they was a makin' them go west, over where the sun set. The Indians thought that was where the sun went to die of an evenin' and that when a person died that they too followed the sun. That's why they were so afraid. Lord, that pore brave fought like a wild man tryin' to pertect his family. But it done him no good. They took 'em all. All but one little girl about fourteen years. She balled herself up and hid in that highest hole. She was the one that appeared on your great-great-grand-pap's doorstep might near froze to death and plumb starved down to nothin'. She lived with him and his family 'till his wife died, and then she married him. That's where you got the Indian blood from. That pore little girl grew to be your great-great-grandma."

I looked way up on the face of the rock and stared at the highest of the seven holes. My great-great-grandma? In that little hole?

"We best be gittin' back, Grandbaby. By the time we git back to the house your Ma will have supper fixed. Hit'll be dark as it is," Breaddaddy said.

We walked out the ridge single file, and right before we moved into the dark woods, I turned and looked back at the rocks rising silently into the gathering twilight, their gray bulk so unnatural there on the tree-covered ridge. I shuddered slightly – a cat must've walked over my grave – then I turned and ran after Breaddaddy, who was just moving out of sight into the woods.

Grubbing Out the Stump

Breaddaddy's mother was named Betty. Her maiden name was Ray, and she came to Sodom as a bride just a few years after the War Between the States ended. She had grown up in the small community called Bull Creek and met my grandpap, Tete Norton, at a box-supper where he had gone to play fiddle. He paid a twenty-dollar gold piece for her supper and managed to make her furious because he bought it right out of the hands of what was then her boyfriend. She wound up dumping the contents in his lap and storming off. He told his cousin that he intended to marry that little redhead, and before their marriage ended with her death, she bore him eight children: five girls and three boys.

Everyone, including her daughters and sons-in-law and all her grandchildren, called her Mother. Dellie Chandler Norton, the woman I would later call Granny because she would become the only real grandmother I would ever know, was one of three daughters-in-law. It was from Granny that I learned the following bittersweet story about my great-grandfather and grandmother's ofttimes stormy union.

They built a cabin next to a little branch in the Burton Cove using logs off their land, and it was there that Mother and Grandpap lived, worked, raised their family, and died. They were buried up on the ridge above the homeplace. Mother chose her burying place so she could sit and look out over the cove and look after her young'uns. You see, Mother married Grandpap a week before she turned fourteen years old, so she was in that cove for a long time.

I imagine the work she did every day was hard and seemingly never ending. But, according to Granny, she kept her house clean, kept her young'uns clean and took them to church – and they behaved. And she demanded respect.

She had a temper. She took no sass from anyone, including Grandpap Tete. Granny said she was a tiny thing, barely five feet tall, and that Pap was over six feet. She also said she remembered quarrels between the two of them that would rage far into the night. Some arguments would get so bad that they would divide the house down the middle; Mother on her side and Pap on his, neither would cross the line, but they would holler back and forth. Now, the children could come and go across the line, and it never seemed to bother them in the least.

But Mother also refused to let the sun rise with them still fighting.

The trees that had been cut off their property were huge, virgin things. And there was a stump left standing outside the kitchen door. Pap kept threatening to hitch his mule team to it and drag it out, but during their marriage, he never got around to it. I think it had to do with self-preservation on his part because that old stump played an important role in their marriage.

Granny said many was the morning, sometimes before daybreak, that you'd see Mother out with her hoe hacking at that stump. She left the hoe sitting right outside the kitchen door, and when things reached a certain point with her and Grandpap's argument, out the door she'd dash, grab that hoe, and commence to digging. Sometimes Pap would stand in the door watching, never saying a word, until, wet with sweat, she would weary and prop the hoe against the house, and the two of them would disappear into the house and close the door.

It must've worked because the two of them lived together for over sixty years.

On the evening of the day Grandpap laid Mother in the earth, he came home from the graveyard, hitched his mules up to the stump, and labored far into the night.

The next morning, the stump was gone and so was Mother's hoe.

Granny Cloe

I don't know if she was crazy or if it was that cap and ball pistol slug she had in her head. I'm talking about my great-grandmother, Cloe Stanton Adams. She was eleven years old when Old Dad, her daddy, shot her in the head. The story goes that she was sent to carry food out to a dugout in the woods where Old Dad was hiding during the Civil War. He thought it was somebody trying to slip up on him, and he shot her. Her brother John was fit to be tied and told Old Dad that he "better hit your knees and pray that Little Cloe lives through this 'cause if she don't, I'm a gonna kill you!" Well, she lived through it and later married my great-grandfather, Neil Adams.

Cloe was a tiny woman. She stood not more than five feet tall and remained slender till the year she died in 1925. She was first generation American. Her father came from Germany and she always said she was "part Black Dutch and part German."

She married my Pap Neil and had two children: Andrew, my grandfather, and Fanny, my great-aunt. The stories told to me by family members paint her as strong willed, independent, outspoken, and crazy as a loon. For instance, she once went for three months without saying a single word. When asked why she did this, she answered, "I was just tired of hearin' myself talk." And another time, one early spring, she decided to take care of the crows that plagued her garden. She sat patiently sewing a short length of thread through the middle of each kernel she intended to plant. After the planting she sat on her porch and watched as the big birds dug up the corn, ate the kernels, and then literally kicked their own heads off trying to do away with the string hanging out of their beaks. There was something about her that just wasn't right – and it seemed to get worse as she got older. It's a pretty much accepted fact that there was something wrong with her mind, so I set about to discover what led folks to believe this.

Poor old Pap Neil seemed to be the one that wound up with the bad end of the stick with Granny Cloe and her rages. Based on family recollections, it was pretty much undeserved. He was a calm, quiet, hardworking man that came into Sodom after the Civil War. He was born down in Cleveland County and came here a young man. There was some dark aspect about his past that has never really been solved. All I know is that he left Cleveland County, came to Sodom, married Granny Cloe, and dearly paid for whatever it was for the rest of his days.

Talk was that after him and Cloe had been married several years, a young man showed up at their door looking for Neil Adams. He found Granny Cloe there by herself, and she invited him in – mainly because she said he looked just like Pap. They talked for a while and she finally asked him why exactly he was looking for Neil. He looked at her for a full minute and never said a word. Finally, he sighed great big and said, " 'Cause I reckon he's my Pap." Granny Cloe took him by the arm, led him out on the porch, and pointed out toward the field across the branch and said, "Then, you see that son of a bitch out there? That's your Pap. Go on and talk to the one that needs to hear this. I got to ask you one thing, though. Does he have another wife stuck out of the way somewheres?" To that the young man answered, "No, Mam, I'm a baseborn." And Cloe answered, "Well, better that than a newly declared orphan."

The boy went out across the field and talked to Pap a long time all hunkered down. Then he came back across the branch, turned left down the road, and was never seen or heard from again. Granny Cloe asked Pap about him, and Pap strongly denied that he was the boy's father. Given the situation and who he had to go to bed with every night, I think I would've denied it too.

She was given to fits of temper that would last for days,

then she would go into a depression that would sometimes last for a month. It was during a couple of these rages that she come close to killing Pap.

The first time was one winter when her and Pap had been housed up together for days. Pap was having a time trying to keep it warm enough in the house to suit her. The rage built to a dangerous level, and Pap escaped the only way he could: he went to bed. Cloe's brother John stopped by and realized she had one of her spells on her. He was sitting at the table with her trying to "devil" her out of it, when, all of a sudden, Granny Cloe got real quiet and narrowed her eyes to slits. She looked at John, and he later said the look in her eyes weren't natural. She stood and walked over to the fire-board and picked up an inkwell, turned back to John, and said, "You see that damned Neil Adams a layin' there?" And John answered, "Why, I reckon I do." And Granny Cloe drew back with all her strength and let that inkwell fly across the room, where it struck Pap square on the temple. It gave him a concussion and came near to killing him. He was out cold for hours.

John said Cloe walked over, picked up the inkwell where it lay on the floor next to the bed, carried it carefully back and placed it on the fire-board, then went to the stove and started making coffee. She turned to John, who still sat at the table in shock, smiled, and said, "How's Nancy's baby? I bet it's really a growin'."

Her second bad fit occurred when her and Pap were both near the end of their lives. Pap was sitting in front of the fireplace with his feet stretched out to the fire, and Granny Cloe was cooking supper. She picked a cast iron frying pan up off the stove, walked up behind him, and hit him in the back of the head with it. He fell over into the floor and lay there for God knows how long before he was discovered by a neighbor. When Granny Cloe was asked later why she hit him, she answered, "I just got mad a lookin' at him a settin' there."

All the female members of the family said she got crazy

when the change of life started up on her. From the stories, though, it sounds like she was that way long before that. Also, there's that Stanton thing. I talked to my cousin Jerry Adams about this part of our family. I admitted to him that most of the stuff I had gleaned about Granny Cloe gave evidence that she probably *was* crazy. But this didn't necessarily mean that all the Stantons were in fact crazy. Did it?

Jerry thought for a while.

"Well," he said, "Daddy and Uncle Wayne talk about Old Dad in his final years leaving his wife, Biddy Stroud, and marrying a younger woman named Liza King. Then Biddy made an apron for one Siddy Franklin and gave it to her with instructions that she was to take Old Dad from Liza. Siddy succeeded in her mission. Then she married him herself and later left him high and dry (this was also part of the apron deal). Old Dad mourned for Siddy the rest of his life and used to sit out on the porch and say over and over, 'Lord, send Siddy and come. Lord, send Siddy and come. Lord, send Siddy and come.'

"And then there was Big William that was always up to mean tricks. He would push unsuspecting folks into a blazing fireplace and then jump in and help beat out the resulting flames, saying, 'Why Lord have mercy! Let me help ye! You've got to be more careful. Don't you know fire'll burn?'

"And then there was Sis. She was over the bank milking the cow, and her husband, Link, was sitting on the porch cleaning fish. The cat came up and, excited by the fish smell, used Link's leg as a scratching post. Link walked almost to the edge of the bank and put that cat to flight. Sis looked up, saw that cat come sailing over, and ran screaming to the barn. She allowed as to how it must be the end of time. She swore that old cat of hers had set into flying like a bird!"

OK. There is some evidence that it might have been a family trait to be a little off. I was still unconvinced.

Jerry sat silent. "You know that graveyard across from old man Ed Shelton's house?" he finally asked.

"Yeah," I said, wondering where in the world this was going now.

"Well, it's just full of Stantons," he stated matter-of-factly, "and not a single one of them died of natural causes."

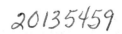

The Easter Frock

Bertha Franklin used to love to sit on her porch and tell me stories about what Sodom was like back when she was a girl. I was always spellbound. Bertha was a great story-teller, and she was the same age as my mother. Her stories formed a window for me, a window I could look through back into the times of my mother as a young girl and young woman.

Evidently, Bertha's mother told her stories about what it was like growing up in Sodom back at the turn of the century. This is a story Bertha told me that her mother, Tootie, told her.

Back then, a peddler drove a horse-drawn wagon around to the different communities, and you could buy just about anything you needed off his wagon. You could get nails, buckets, and dry goods. You could even buy cloth.

Before Easter one year, Tootie managed to save up enough money to buy a pretty piece of filmy material to make herself an Easter frock to wear to church. Now, back then, the dresses had a bustle on them that stuck out over the hind end. If you could afford it you could buy a wire frame to make it stand out, but if you couldn't, well, you just stuffed it with rags.

Tootie spent a lot of time working on her frock and finished it the Saturday night before Easter Sunday. She hung it on the back of the door and went on to bed thinking how pretty she'd look next day at church.

She got up late the next morning and realized she had forgotten to stuff her bustle the night before. She hurriedly reached in the rag bag, pulled out an old flour sack, and commenced to stuffing that bustle.

She got to church and swept right down to the front, holding that dress tail out, nodding and smiling and speaking to everybody.

As soon as folks stood for the first hymn, Tootie heard some snickering behind her. And every hymn thereafter, it seemed like the snickering spread till it was all the way to the very back of the church.

When the last amen was said, Tootie hit the door. She checked to see if her slip was hanging or if all her buttons were buttoned, but she couldn't find a single thing undone. She stiffened her spine and stormed off down the road.

About halfway home, her brothers caught up with her and just set into horse laughing, all doubled over holding their sides. Tootie, who had a temper to match her shining red hair, had suffered enough in silence. She wheeled around on them boys with a vengeance.

"I want to know what's so damn funny?" she said. "Folks has laughed at me all morning in church, and I'm about sick of it!"

But you know how brothers are (and Tootie was blessed with eight of them). They just laughed even harder and ran off down the road with Tootie chucking rocks at them as hard as she could.

By this time I reckon Tootie was livid! She charged down the road, marched up the hill to the house, and slammed through the door, banging it closed behind her hard enough to rattle all the window glasses in the house. She started down the hall to her room and spied the hall chair sitting there – the one with the mirror on the wall above it. She climbed up on the chair, positioned herself so she could look over her shoulder, and there across her bustle you could read, plain as day: "50 LBS. OF THE VERY BEST."

[17]

Traitor

Breaddaddy was a real looker when he was a young man. This is based on old photographs and what all the older women in Sodom have told me. Granny says he had the bluest eyes she'd ever seen then or since. Also according to Granny, he never suffered from a lack of female attention.

Ma used to laugh and tell this story.

Breaddaddy had a mule named Little Pete. He was as stubborn as Breaddaddy, and you could hear them, man and mule, yelling and braying all over the Burton Cove. But I think Breaddaddy really had a deep respect for Little Pete. I reckon Pete was one of the only creatures on earth that he couldn't bend to his will.

Breaddaddy would ride Pete down to the store of an evening. He went pretty much every evening to talk with other folks that gathered at the store at the end of the day. Ma never thought much about it. Every other man she knew in the community went, so why not Breaddaddy?

One warm spring evening, Breaddaddy announced that he had promised to help drive a herd of hogs out to Greeneville, Tennessee, the next day. He would be leaving early the next morning and would be gone all day and night. Ma allowed as to how that was fine and she would give him a list of things he could get for her out in Greeneville.

The next morning, with Ma's list tucked in his pocket and a lunch under his arm, he headed down the road with his herding stick resting on his shoulder. Ma was left with the young'uns, everything to do, and Little Pete.

Down in the day, Ma realized she needed to go to the store and get a little sugar. She said she was wore out, so she decided to saddle Little Pete up and save herself a walk. By the time she got Pete in his harness it was around the time Breaddaddy usually took his trip in the evenings.

Ma climbed on Pete's back, and they started off down the road. Things went pretty good until they got right even with a little road that led up to a house there in the community. And that's where Little Pete made an unexpected detour. He carried Ma right up to the steps and stood, ears twitching, waiting. Ma just turned him around and went back down the road toward the store.

The next evening when Breaddaddy got home I'm sure he got a right interesting welcome.

My uncle Byard said that later on that week he stopped in to see Breaddaddy, and Ma said, "He's down in the barn with Little Pete, and as fer as I care, he can stay there permanent."

Well, Byard said he eased down to the barn and he could hear Breaddaddy talking back there in the semidarkness. Byard stood right quiet and listened.

"I just want to know whatever you could've been a thinkin', you durn fool mule? I know me an' you, we've had our differences, but now they just ain't no excuse fer turnin' on me that a way. And don't you go a tryin' to let on like you couldn't tell a difference twixt mine and Emily's weight. You done that little trick a takin' her up to that t'other woman's house out a meanness and spite, and now you've done got me in a big ole pile a' trouble. Don't you shake your head at me. I know you, you rascal. Just like that time you stepped on my foot and durn near crippled me. And now this! Well, I'm sick an' tired of you! I'm a gonna change your name, I'll fix you proper."

Byard said he was having a hard time trying to keep from laughing by this time, so he called out and said, "Poppie, are you in there? Who're you talking to?"

There was a brief silence, and then Breaddaddy told Byard to come on back. Byard asked if anything was wrong with Little Pete. Breaddaddy looked disgustedly over at the mule and said, "No, I don't reckon, but don't be callin' this no account, poor excuse for a beast of labor Little Pete. I've changed his name."

"To what, Poppie?" Byard asked.

And Breaddaddy said in all seriousness, "I'm gonna brand his name right on his rump so ever'body can read it plain. I'm renamin' this varmint Traitor!"

Breaddaddy called Little Pete "Traitor" for a long time. Byard said you could hear Breaddaddy yelling, "Gee, Traitor, Haw!" all over the Burton Cove. And Byard said Little Pete would cut his eyes around at Breaddaddy with a look of pure glee and amusement.

By the time I came along, Little Pete was back to being Little Pete, and he and Breaddaddy were on better terms. They had only one argument when Breaddaddy called him Traitor that I can recall. I asked why he'd called him that.

Breaddaddy looked at Little Pete, grinned, and said, "Hit's a lot of water under the bridge, Grandbaby. And better left alone."

Little Pete outlived Breaddaddy by almost two years. After Breaddaddy died, Pete wandered the fields, picking grass and just resting. I'm sure he missed his lifelong friend.

George Foster and the Haint

I used to play in the Presbyterian graveyard when I was a child. It had been established sometime in the early 1900s and was taken up by the Presbyterians in the 1920s. I'm sure this bothered the Baptists that had loved ones buried there, because everyone knows that them Presbyterians believe that you're either saved when you're born or you ain't, and most folks in Sodom felt that if they couldn't get "forgiveness" on a pretty regular basis, then all was indeed lost.

Anyway, the fact that it was owned and maintained by the Presbyterians didn't bother us young'uns in the least. But the haint tales did. One of the most hair-raising tales came from my great-uncle Herb Lester.

Years ago the men would slip off and play poker. They would often play in someone's barn until the womenfolk found out where they were playing, and then they would take their blanket and move somewhere else. In the summertime they could often be found playing by lantern light underneath the stars.

This night, they were playing next to the graveyard in what we always called the Old Road, which was no longer used. The Old Road ran right beside the graveyard. Herb and a big crowd of local men were gathered around an old blanket, with four or five lanterns setting around to provide light. One of the men said he had to relieve himself and left the circle and climbed a ways up the path to the graveyard. The men played on for a while, and then a great scream split the quiet, and they all heard the man start running. He was screaming something awful.

"It's after me, it's after me!" he kept screaming.

Of course, all the men stood up and grabbed their lanterns, holding them above their heads to try and see what in the world was going on. Herb said the man come a runnin' by them with a look of pure horror on his face.

Then one of the men said, "What in the Hell is that?" as he pointed to the path.

Herb said it looked like somebody had unfolded a news-paper and spread it out flat, but he said it wasn't laying on the ground. It was hovering about three feet off the ground and looked like it was waving in the wind – only there was no wind on this hot summer night. He said the night was still as any he'd ever seen. Not even the katydids was singing.

Then Herb said whatever it was started to move, slowly at first, coming down the path toward them. Herb said all he could think to do was to bring the lantern he was hold-ing up over his head and throw it with all his power at the damn thing. He said the lantern went right through it and landed on the path, where the glass shattered.

When this happened, the men scattered in all different directions. There was a full moon that night, and Herb said he ran just so far, then turned to see where the thing had gone. George Foster, one of the men just standing around watching the game that night, was running full speed down the Old Road screaming, "Don't let it git me God!"

Herb and his wife, my great-aunt Flossie, had taken in George Foster, who was not from Sodom, years ago. His real family didn't want him because he was sort of simple-minded, or so they said. But he had grown up there in Sodom and was accepted as one of us. He was also a big help to Flossie and Herb now that their own sons had moved away from home.

Herb said that he thought George would've been able to get away if he'd only been quiet. But when he ran scream-ing, Herb said the thing kind of shuddered and turned like it heard him or something. And then it took out after him. Herb said whatever it was, it was evil. He said the air was thick with it. It smelled like rubber burning.

But George Foster was running and screaming and cry-ing. It was right behind him. All of a sudden it rose, and Herb said when it was right behind his head it looked like it bumped him three times on the back of the neck. George screamed such an awful scream that Herb said he bit his own lip till he tasted blood, just to keep from crying out. That's when he began to run, too.

By the time Herb got home, George was already there sitting on the porch and moaning like some kind of hurt animal. My great-aunt was out there with him trying to comfort him and trying to get him to tell her what was the matter.

All he could say was, "It burned me, it burned me."

Herb and Flossie finally got him in the kitchen. Flossie pulled up his shirt, and there were three paper thin blisters across the back of his neck. Herb said they were all in a line and exactly the same size. Flossie doctored them and then sent George upstairs to go to bed. Flossie didn't put much faith in what Herb or George had said because she figured they had been drinking.

The next day, all the men gathered up and went back to see if they could find anything. They found nothing except for their broken lanterns and their quilt, which was just as they had left it – money, cards, and all.

George nursed his neck for several days, saying it was the most painful thing he'd ever had, and Flossie doctored it as best she could. It healed in a couple of weeks and left three thin red scars. After a month or so, folks forgot. Except for Herb and the other men. They never played cards there again.

And George Foster? Well, he died in a car wreck three months to the day after that. The car caught fire and he was burned beyond recognition.

The Ghost Dog

During the Great War, as it's called over home, there was a Rebel soldier who got set upon by some Yankees and was killed way back up in the Gudger Tract. Traveling with him was a big white shepherd dog. The Yanks tried to catch it, even shot at it a few times, but the dog managed to get away. The Yanks buried the Rebel there and moved on.

But the dog stayed.

For years, folks who passed back and forth through that area saw it there around the grave. Some folks tried to call the dog to them, but it would only sit watching, never straying too far from the grave site of its master.

Some years later the dog was found dead, lying right across the grave. Someone dug a hole and buried it beside the man it had guarded even after death.

Then came stories from reliable folks about a great white dog that would trot along by your side for a ways as you walked or rode your horse along the path that wound around the ridge. The place became known as Rebel Ridge and is still called that today.

George Bishop was one of those who swore he had seen the dog.

George had a bit to drink and had laid out just about all night playing cards. He figured his wife was waiting up for him just so she could give him a good cussing, so he decided to take a shortcut up along Rebel Ridge. He came out on top of the ridge and started out along the path, picking his way by the light of a full moon. He said he wasn't even thinking about no dog, just the cussing he was in for, when all of a sudden, right there beside him, trotting along, was the biggest white dog he had ever seen. He said, "Git from here!" and kicked at it, thinking to run it off. But much to his surprise, his foot went clear through it.

He stopped dead in his tracks and took a good look at it.

All the hairs on the back of his neck stood straight up. He said later if he had've had any hair on his head it wouldn't have fit in a bushel basket, because what he saw almost scared him to death. The dog had glowing red eyes, and George could see the ground right through it. He decided right then that something un-natural was a taking place and he broke to run.

He was "a pickin' 'em up and a puttin' 'em down" and the dog stayed right with him. Much to his horror, the dog looked up and said, plain as any person might, "We a runnin' now, ain't we?"

This stunned George so bad that he stopped, clutching his breast, gasping for breath. The dog stopped too and sat looking up at him. "We a restin' now, ain't we?" the dog asked.

George started to run again with the dog loping along beside him. "We a runnin' again, ain't we?" the dog asked.

George was pretty much blind with fear by now, so it's no wonder that he didn't see the root across the path until his foot caught on it, sprawling him face down in the dirt.

He pulled his coat up over his head and lay real still, expecting at any minute to feel the dog's teeth sink into his leg or his arm. After a few minutes, when his breathing and his heart slowed down, he dared a peek out from under his coat.

Sure enough, there sat the dog, patiently watching him. "We a restin' again, ain't we?"

Well, George figured he had just about had enough of this. He looked the dog square in them ole red eyes and said, "Yes, aye God, we are. And when we're good and rested, then we're gonna git up and run some damn more!"

George lived to tell his tale, and as far as I know, he never took the nigh way home across Rebel Ridge again.

The Christmas Miracle

My mother says that Old Christmas is celebrated on January 7th. Our family celebrated Christmas on December 25. That was when Santy Claus came. I always had plenty on Christmas morning, even though I had not necessarily been a "good girl." My best Christmas took place on Old Christmas Eve when I was a little girl, five years old.

My mother taught school, and my grandmother kept me during the day while Mama worked. Occasionally, especially if bad weather was a possibility, I had to spend the night. This night turned out to be one of those times. There was a cold north wind blowing that cut to the bone, and a freezing mixture of snow and needle-sharp sleet was falling.

Breaddaddy had entertained me all evening long with stories about the baby Jesus. He'd given me his version of the Bible story about Jesus being born in a stable with the cold wind whistling around the barn. He compared the weather to what we were having this night. Breaddaddy took me out into the dark with his old lantern in his hand.

"This," he said, "is the way it was when pore little Mary laid down in the cold straw of that barn and gave birth to the mightiest man that ever lived."

I felt the cold and thought about the little boy being born, naked and freezing, so many years ago. My heart swelled and hurt for him.

Breaddaddy picked me up and carried me back inside the warmth of the house, where Ma waited with hands on her hips to scold us, "Bob, whatever are you a thinkin'? Takin' her out'na weather not fit fer a dog. She'll catch a sickness sure'n the world."

Breaddaddy pulled his chair close to the stove and rocked me back and forth to the sound of the clock ticking.

I began to feel sleepy, but I begged for one more story, and this is what he told me.

"The night of our Savior's birth was so very special that it was almost magic. Shepherds on the hillside were told by many angels about the happenin', and they hurried to see this wonderful child. Wisemen followed a blazin' star to see Him and to bring Him gifts and riches. Now, not just the people in the world had been waitin', but the animals had been waitin' too. And the animals 'knew' somehow when He gave his birth cry. They knew He was the special promise. And at the very moment of His birth there was a great flutter and racket that rose from the animals everywhere in the world. The chickens flapped their wings and crowed, even the hens crowed! The dogs barked and howled. The cats sat on their haunches and squalled and hollered. The great elephants in Africa raised their mighty trunks and squealed their welcome. The bears roared and stood on their hind legs, even the birds and snakes sang and hissed. Every animal joined in with their special sound to make the baby feel welcome. And then, almost as if by some secret signal only animals could hear with their keen ears, they each and every one stopped their racket and cocked their head to one side like they was listenin'. The animals began to kneel down – all over the world, all the animals settled to the ground and lowered their heads like they was prayin'. I bet even the fish settled to the bottom of the rivers.

"And that miracle still takes place all around the world on Old Christmas Eve, which is what tonight is. So, at midnight tonight, in just four hours, all the animals will kneel just like they've done for hundreds of years."

You can just imagine the wonderful picture this painted in my mind. I could just see old Tippy and Chippy, my grandfather's fox hounds, kneeling on the cold ground, and the chickens lowering their heads. But even more beautiful in my mind was the vision of Kate and Pete, Breaddaddy's mules down in the barn, kneeling. I fell asleep with those thoughts in my mind.

It seemed like seconds later I was awakened by gentle hands lifting me from a warm bed and a voice whispering in my ear. "Be real quiet now, Grandbaby, and don't wake your Ma. She won't let us do what I aim to do if she wakes up and catches us." Needless to say, I never said a word.

Breaddaddy dressed me in my warm clothes that he had laid over a chair next to the stove, and bundled me up in one of Ma's warm quilts. We slipped out the door into a cold and vast silence. He lit the lantern, and I could see the huge snowflakes falling within the circle of yellow light cast by the flame. He adjusted the wick and swept me back into the warm curve of his arm, and we began to make our way carefully to the barn. Only when we reached the barn door did I dare to speak. "What time is it, Breaddaddy?" I asked after he had set me down alongside the lantern and turned to close and bolt the barn door.

He reached down in the front pocket of his overalls and pulled out the watch he kept there. He flipped open the lid covering the face and said, "Hit's about eight minutes till midnight."

He picked up the lantern and headed to the back of the barn, where Kate and Pete and the milk cow were stabled. I followed with Ma's quilt dragging in the dusty dirt of the barn.

I heard Breaddaddy speak softly to the mules and heard Pete answer him with the sound only Pete made. I heard the scraping sound that meant Kate had lifted her head over the bars of the door, and in the dim light I could see Breaddaddy with his blue wool hat pulled down over his ears patting Kate's nose. Their warm breath plumed like smoke in the cold air. I saw Breadddaddy reach into his pocket and start to pull out his watch. And now, this is where, if he hadn't talked about it years later, I would've wondered if my child's mind had created the whole thing.

I can see it all clearly, even now. Kate pulled her head back in the stall, and Pete made his peculiar whickering sound, and the cow mooed softly from her pen. Breaddaddy raised his lantern high above his head, his watch dangling forgotten on its leather strip. There was a look of pure wonder on his face.

"Come quick, Grandbaby," he said softly, "hurry!"

I shrugged out of the quilt and ran to his side. He took my arm and brought my face closer to the bars of the stable, and I looked in.

Pete and Kate had both settled to the ground! Their heads were lowered to where their noses almost touched the dirt. Breaddaddy whirled and almost ran the few feet to the cow's pen. I followed on his heels. The cow was also kneeling with lowered head! And without a single word between us, my grandfather and I kneeled in the clean dirt of the barn.

I reckon the moment had some real magic to it. One memory stands clear: As we made our way back to the house, we stopped, and I stood with my hand in Breaddaddy's. We turned our faces up into the dark silence that was the sky and stood briefly as the snow covered our shoulders.

Years later, after Ma died, Breaddaddy walked down from the Burton Cove one day to stay with me because I had the measles and couldn't go to school. I was in the fourth grade then. He pulled a chair close to my bed and was telling me stories from the Bible about Samson.

"Breaddaddy," I interrupted. "Do you remember one Old Christmas Eve I spent with you and Ma when you took me to the barn at midnight?"

He looked at me with eyes of purest blue. "Oh yes, Grandbaby, I remember," he said.

"Did it really happen?" I asked.

"Yes, Grandbaby, it happened," Breaddaddy said. "It was a miracle me and you shared that night. A real miracle."

Taking Jete Home

Breaddaddy saw the car right at daylight. He had left the house headed for the barn to feed. He came running back into the kitchen, where Ma was getting her milk buckets ready, and I sat at the table eating my oatmeal.

"They's a car settin' pulled over next to the buckeye tree. Looks like they's three people in it. I think it's Jete, Willard, and Josh. The engines a runnin', and the snow has banked up agin' the tail pipe. None of 'em's movin'. You'll need to run up to Will's and tell 'em to come quick."

Breaddaddy said all this as he stood next to the door, the snow from his boots forming a puddle around his feet. I watched as a small stream started to snake out toward the middle of the floor.

Ma was hurriedly putting on her coat, hat, and gloves. She never wore pants. She had on a thick pair of socks that disappeared up under her dress tail.

"I'll go git Nellie. I don't know that Will is able to come. He's been awful sick."

Ma's voice trailed off as her and Breaddaddy went out and closed the door. I sat there at the table, oatmeal changing to glue in my blue enamel bowl. The house was so quiet and still, I jumped when the eight-days clock chimed out. I counted seven chimes. I pushed myself out of the chair and went into the living room, where my clothes were spread neatly on the ladder-back chair next to the stove.

Breaddaddy had the door on the driver's side open by the time I walked out on the porch. I could hear him talking above the running engine from where I stood. He reached in, and suddenly the engine stilled, and all I could hear was the little branch that ran down on the other side of the road.

I stepped off the porch and the snow came to right above my four-year-old knees. I walked stiff-legged, pushing the snow ahead of me like a plow. When I got to the end of the yard, I looked back at the two perfectly straight lines leading back to the porch and smiled. I turned and looked back at Breaddaddy when I heard voices riding on the cold, snowy air. I saw Nellie and Ma coming down the road. They were almost running over the ice- and snow-covered road, and I could hear Aunt Nellie saying over and over, "Oh Lord, please. Oh Lord, please. Oh Lord, please."

Aunt Nellie climbed in the front seat and took the head of the man behind the wheel between her two hands. I watched as she encircled his shoulders and pulled him to her breast and rocked her body back and forth, smoothing the hair on the back of his head with her hand.

Ma stood next to the open door, her hands dangling from her sleeves. She turned to Breaddaddy and said, "Go hitch up the mules to the sled. We've got to git 'em out of there."

Breaddaddy headed to the barn. He slipped on the slick road and almost fell. I smiled as he regained his balance.

I squatted down in the road, peeping into the car, where Aunt Nellie still rocked, back and forth, back and forth. Ma talked softly to her as she, bent from the waist, leaned into the car.

When Breaddaddy returned with the sled, Ma said softly, "Git out now, Nellie. Bob's come with the sled and we're gonna move Jete out now. We'll need you to help us. Come on, git out, honey."

No sound from Aunt Nellie as she rocked Jete.

Ma looked helplessly at Breaddaddy, who sighed and held the reins out in Ma's direction. She moved toward his outstretched hand and took the lines.

He walked to the open door and squatted down next to the car. He was talking too low for me to hear. I turned my head and looked at the mules. Their breath puffed out, making smoke, and I could see ice forming around their mouths as they chewed and worked at the bit.

I looked back at the car. Aunt Nellie got out and leaned against the snowcapped top and rested her head on her arm.

"Nellie, we need you to help us git him out of there. Come on now, help us."

Breaddaddy looked at Ma and nodded. Ma glanced down at the lines in her hand and for the first time noticed me squatted in the snow.

"Come hold these lines, Sealy," she said.

I rose and walked stiff-legged to her, and she placed the reins in my small hand.

"Don't hold 'em too loose now, and stand still."

I stood as told.

Aunt Nellie, Ma, and Breaddaddy wrestled Jete from the car and carried him over to the sled. Breaddaddy took the reins from me and told me to get up at the front. I climbed on beside Jete and settled myself next to his head.

Breaddaddy slapped the reins against the back of the two mules, and they moved out up the road in perfect unison. Aunt Nellie and Ma walked behind the sled, Ma's arm draped across Aunt Nellie's shoulders.

I looked down at Jete. Snow had collected on his face, and I brushed it away. His head rolled with the movement of the sled and came to rest against my leg. I put my hand on his cheek and held it there so it wouldn't move.

They carried Jete into Aunt Nellie's warm kitchen and laid him out on the table. Aunt Nellie filled up a pan with warm water and set it next to him.

"No Nellie," Ma said. "Let me do that. Lord, there ain't no need in you doin' that. Leave it."

I gazed up into Aunt Nellie's still face. Her eyes were so shiny looking and so full of pain that I felt my own heart tighten, and my eyes burned with tears.

"No," she said in a soft voice as she squeezed the water from the rag. "I'll do it myself. I got to. This is the last time I'll ever get to wash my baby."

Ma watched with tears running down her face, wringing the old pillowcase in her hands.

Aunt Nellie looked at me and smiled. "Sealy, git that rag from your Ma and tear it into long strips fer me."

I took the rag from Ma's still-working hands and pulled

me a chair over to sit closer to the stove. I made sure to tear the strips long for Aunt Nellie. I loved Aunt Nellie and wanted to please her.

"Bring them here, honey," Aunt Nellie said as she finished washing Jete's face. I scooted out of the chair and held out one of the strips. Aunt Nellie took it and wrapped it around underneath Jete's chin and tied it securely on top of his head. "Help me git his shirt off, Emily."

Ma and Aunt Nellie removed his shirt, and I watched as Aunt Nellie washed his chest and arms, her touch gentle.

They made me leave the room a bit later, and I sat in the living room playing with one of Aunt Nellie's cats.

Through that whole long morning while we waited for the undertaker to come from Marshall to get Jete, I played with the cats and watched the snow blow outside the window. I was finally allowed back into the kitchen, where Jete lay in clean clothes and Aunt Nellie fed me a jelly biscuit.

I don't remember the funeral. I don't remember Aunt Nellie crying. I do remember her standing beside the newly covered grave, clutching her arms around her middle like she was holding her grief inside by mere physical force.

When Ma Died

Although it may sound morbid to some folks, I wish the old-fashioned wake still took place here in the mountains. Used to be when a person died, the family took them in to the funeral home located in the county seat. After the departed loved one was fixed up, he or she was hauled back home and set up there to await burial. During this waiting period friends and relatives would come to sit up with the body. Lots of times a wake took on the air of a family reunion. Of course, there was grief and mourning, but it was an open, cleansing type of mourning – and what better place than with loving relatives and friends? Just about everyone in the community turned out to offer support, to bring food, and to socialize.

I attended many wakes as a child, and it was at one of those old mountain wakes that I learned about and accepted death as a part of life. I learned it while sitting in my mother's lap, feeling warm and secure in my grandparents home.

My grandmother on my mother's side was a wonderfully warm and gentle soul. She was the kind of person forever inviting folks to "come in and set a spell and I'll fix us a cup of coffee, and we'll eat some of this cake I just baked."

My first cousin Sharon and I spent the first five years of our lives with Ma. She baby-sat while our mothers worked. Sharon and I had our first taste of snuff and tobacco there when we sneaked down to the spring house and helped ourselves to some from the box we had "borrowed" from Ma. She found us out, too, because both of us turned a pale shade of green. Ma let us help with all her chores. I learned to wash on a rub board, churn butter, and wind the old clock that sat on the dresser.

We loved being with Ma and Breaddaddy so much that we also spent days there that our mothers didn't work. This particular day we were there on a Saturday morning sitting in front of the TV watching cartoons. Ma came into the living room from the kitchen and sat down in her rocking chair with a sigh. She said she didn't feel quite right. Seconds later she began struggling for breath, and there in her chair, she died. Sharon and I looked over at Ma when she began making funny noises, and when her body relaxed, we stood up and went over to her. I asked Sharon if Ma was snoring, and Sharon looked at me and said, "No, I think Ma's dead."

We ran to the couch where Breaddaddy was sleeping and woke him and said, "Breaddaddy, something has happened to Ma."

I still didn't understand, even though the tears sprang to Breaddaddy's eyes and he told us to run and get Nora, Sharon's mother.

I remember running up the road to Sharon's house, wondering what in the world had happened. On the way we passed my father in his car. Sharon told him that Ma had died and Breaddaddy had sent her to get her Mama. Daddy told us to go on to Nora's and stay there until he came to get us. Although I usually did what Daddy said without question, this was one time I refused. And this was one time he didn't whip me for disobeying. I got in the car with him, and we drove back to Breaddaddy's. I followed Daddy into the house and into the living room. Breaddaddy stood by Ma's chair holding her hand and crying. Daddy went over and gently moved Breaddaddy aside and leaned over Ma. It was then he remembered me. He looked at me and then at Breaddaddy.

"I'm gonna move her into the bedroom, Bob," he said.

Breaddaddy nodded, and Daddy picked her up and carried her to the next room and laid her on her bed.

When he came back into the living room, he pointed at me and said, "Do not go in the bedroom."

I recognized his "you better do as I say or else" tone of voice. I nodded.

Things at this point become hazy. I remember Nora coming, and then my mother and their brother Arthur. My mother sent me home with my older sister, and when we all went back the next evening, Ma was set up in the living room in her coffin.

The living room was full of people. The funeral home had left folding chairs for all the company to use. And, of course, we all spent the night. Sharon and I were sent to bed upstairs early. We played and talked awhile, and then we heard Mama and Nora crying.

"Why are they cryin'?" I asked Sharon.

"Cause Ma is dead," Sharon answered solemnly.

Long after Sharon was asleep, I stared up into the darkened rafters pondering her words in my heart.

I woke several hours later and could hear people talking softly downstairs. I decided this had gone on long enough and figured it was up to me to do something about it. I slipped quietly down the narrow stairs and peeked into the living room. No one was in the room with Ma, so I walked up to the side of the coffin and looked over the side. She was so still that for an instant I hesitated, but I finally reached out and touched her cheek.

"Ma?" I whispered, for although the room was empty save for Ma and me, I could hear the soft voices coming from the kitchen. "You need to git up now. There's a big bunch of people here, and they're just a eatin' and a gommin'. I know you don't feel too good, but you'll feel better if you just git up and see all this company. Git up now, Ma. Please."

I heard a gasp behind me and turned to see my pregnant first cousin standing in the doorway. She called to Mama, and Mama came into the room. When my cousin told Mama what she'd heard, Mama crossed the room and took me in her arms.

She sat down in Ma's rocker and started to rock me back and forth. She explained how Ma had gone to heaven now and she was very happy and she didn't hurt anymore. She also told me that as long as I could remember Ma in my heart, a tiny part of her would stay alive. I remember I cried for a while, and then the next thing I remember is Sharon waking me and telling me to hurry and get up because we had to start getting ready for the funeral.

We walked up the path to the graveyard above my uncle's house. They buried my grandmother on a hilltop that looks out over the entire valley. Her grave is surrounded by white pines, and when there's a breeze, it sounds as though they're whispering to one another.

You Best Not Nod Off to Sleep

Breaddaddy lived to be eighty-four years old and was a deputy sheriff for the last twenty-five years of his life. I think the High Sheriff appointed him so he could legally carry a gun. He carried one anyway and had never been shy about using it when need be, but at least during his deputy years, he was covered. It came in handy for the High Sheriff of the county more than once, especially the time he had to go up to Chicago to bring back a notorious killer named Evanfeld.

Our county had its share of fights. Sometimes somebody wound up getting knifed or shot. And we had some killings. But they were usually pretty straightforward, and more likely than not, whoever did the killing would turn himself in down at the jail. But what took place in the little community called Creek was not a run-of-the-mill occurrence.

Creek, like Sodom, was an isolated, sleepy little place snuggled up against the Tennessee line. It was like Sodom also in that the main focus of the community was the church and the little general store. It was in this little general store that one of the most bizarre murders the county had ever known took place.

The store was run by an elderly couple, and before that by one of the owner's parents. As with most of the general stores in the county, they closed around nine o'clock each evening and opened whenever they chose in the morning.

There was no sign of forced entry on this particular Saturday morning when the Sheriff got there after receiving a call that something was wrong at the store over in Creek. It was obvious that money had been taken because the cash register hung open and some coins lay scattered around on the floor. It was also obvious that the couple who owned and ran the store were very much dead. They had been placed in two chairs back to back, tied, and had been shot one time each in the head.

The High Sheriff of our county was a very smart lawman. (He had at one time turned down an offer for a position with the F.B.I.) He recognized immediately that the couple had been murdered execution-style. But he was stuck. There were no fingerprints, no clues existed at all. He figured this was a case that would probably remain unsolved. And he proved right, at least for a while.

The call came in from Chicago about a year and a half later. It appeared that the police had picked up three men there and were questioning them about two murders. One of the three decided to turn state's witness and told a tale that even the police up there found hard to imagine.

It seemed these three had been on a robbing and killing spree all over the United States for three years. Their method was to enter a store, rob the place, and leave no witnesses. And, according to this man, one of those places was a little mountain store in western North Carolina.

The High Sheriff decided to make the drive to Chicago and bring the main man back to the county for trial. He needed someone to go with him that he could depend on. He chose my grandfather, an old man even then. Folks around here wondered about the smartness of this move, though years later the High Sheriff told me that he never had a single doubt about Breaddaddy.

The police had Evanfeld in chains when the Sheriff picked him up. They put him in the back seat of the car and warned the Sheriff that this man was extremely dangerous. The Sheriff said, "Oh, I'm not worried. I reckon he'll behave." And then he looked over at Breaddaddy and said, "Keep an eye on him, Bob. If he moves, even slightly, kill him." And with that, they headed home to North Carolina.

Twenty-three hours later, Evanfeld was locked securely in the county jail, and Breaddaddy was sound asleep in his own bed.

The local newspaper came and interviewed Evanfeld. Seems he was pretty well known in the crime world. The reporter asked about his trip down, and after a bit of thought Evanfeld said, "The Sheriff seems to be a reasonable man. We talked quite a bit during the trip. But it was that old gray-haired, blue-eyed man that bothered me. You know, he rode turned around the entire trip. He never once took his eyes off me, and he never spoke a single word after we left Chicago. As a matter of fact he only said one sentence to me the whole trip."

"And what was that?" the reporter asked.

"Well," replied Evanfeld, "as we were leaving the Chicago jail he pulled out his gun, cocked the hammer, and said, 'If you move one inch in either direction I'm a gonna kill you, so you best not nod off to sleep.'"

"And did you doubt what he said?"

"Not for a second," Evanfeld said. "I was awake for the whole trip. And so was that old man."

A Special Dance

Death and dying are pretty much a part of everyday life in Sodom. Either someone actually dies or death's being talked about in that hushed but vibrant tone people over home adopt when they speak of it. It is also the tone of voice they use when talking about women who have female troubles. Comments about someone's death or dying are pretty common:

"Yeah, I saw him yesterday and I thought he looked like Death a eatin' a cracker. I don't think he is long for this world."

"Law, he is in such awful shape. They say he's just wasted down to plumb nothin'."

"You know, he started talkin' about John the other night – just out of the blue, and him been dead for nigh on sixteen years. I've always heard when someone is real sick and they start mentionin' them that has gone on that it won't be long afore they meet 'em in Glory."

The cemetery that was just down the road from my home place was a wonderful playground for me and my cousins. It lay nestled between two ridges and was peaceful and quiet. I was never really frightened while playing there, but I do admit to being uneasy at times. Mainly because of the haint stories the grown-ups told us on cold winter evenings. And then they would scratch their heads in wonder when we woke up screaming a few hours later.

Anyway, one warm summer day I remember watching Breaddaddy and two other men struggle with what appeared to me to be a giant white tombstone. It looked as though they were trying to rip it from the head of the very first grave you came to after you'd left the path leading to the graveyard.

"Whatcha doin'?" I asked my grandfather.

Without looking up he answered, "Movin' the tomb rock over a bit so it won't be right in the main path."

I stood there shaking my head back and forth, liking the feel of my hair brushing against my shoulders and my arms that stuck out like sticks from my sleeveless shirt.

"Are you gonna move the coffin too?" I asked.

Already I could envision the telling of the story to my friends. Maybe, if I was allowed to stay with them, I might get a glimpse of bleached bones or decaying flesh. How exciting, how horrifying! This could definitely raise me to a position of envy among all my cousins in Sodom. Already in my mind's ear I could hear their squeals and groans.

"Move outna th' way, honey child," my grandfather said, interrupting my thoughts of fame, coffins, and what lay within.

I moved back a few steps, and the men wrestled the tombstone into a freshly dug hole on the other side of the path. The two men helping Breaddaddy kneeled to pack the dirt in around it.

"You gonna move the coffin too?" I asked a bit louder.

"Nah," he said. "We're just gonna leave him lay; he'll never know the difference."

"But you ain't supposed to walk on graves! Mama said so. She busted me last year for jumpin' on Uncle Arnol's grave. And that was a week after decoration Sunday. She said she would've killed me if I had've done it Decoration Day, what with all them people watchin'. She said walkin' on graves showed bad disrespect for them that was dead."

The three men laughed, and Breaddaddy took out a dingy white handkerchief and wiped his sweaty face. He looked over at me and smiled. He slowly walked over to where I stood and laid a gentle hand on my shoulder.

"Your Mam's right. You shouldn't walk on graves outen respect for them that's passed on. But we can't move this fella. He's been gone from this world a long time and if'en we tried to move him it'd just be a big gom, what with the coffin all rotted and him a spillin' out the holes. There's probably not much left down there anyways."

He pulled me close, and for a moment I buried my face in his faded work shirt. I breathed in the old-man scent of him – the sweat, the chewing tobacco, and the clean, outdoors smell that always clung to his clothes.

Then he pulled away, patted my head, and winked.

I looked up into his face, and my eyes met his. I saw the laughter breaking up the blueness there beneath his white, bushy brows, and he said, "Far be it from me to let you get away with somethin' your Mam wouldn't let you do."

He held out his hand to me as he began to dance a little jig on the grave. I reached out and placed my hand in his. He began to sing the words to an old familiar fiddle tune, "Cumberland Gap ain't my home and I'm gonna leave old Cumberland alone." I moved my feet in time with his, and we laughed and did a right arm swing, our feet now flying above what remained of a man long gone.

Now, years later and a woman grown, I always pause when I enter that graveyard. A smile spreads across my face. In my mind I can see the two of us as we must've looked. A skinny little girl with brown eyes too big for her face, with the promise of all life had to offer stretching out in front of her, and the old man in his final days, his face tanned and creased with age, and his eyes like blue crystal – dancing. Two children, actually, with the same blood flowing through our veins, and the same song in our hearts. My feet, with a mind of their own, give a shuffle or two, and my heart lifts with the memory of the old man long since fertilizing the graveyard ground there in Sodom.

Minnie Laws and the German Police Dog

Minnie Laws lived in an old two-room log cabin up in the Big Cove. She had lived most of her life right there in that old house, raised her young'uns, and watched them leave one by one for greener pastures. Except for one daughter, Cindy. She stayed home with Minnie and raised her children right there in the same house.

Howard, the welder/electrician son, had done real good. He lived in Knoxville and would visit Minnie there at the family homeplace occasionally. And when he came for a visit, he would bring Minnie something:

A plastic framed picture of the Lord's Supper that you could screw two light bulbs in the back and it would alternately light up horns on Judas' head and a halo around Jesus'.

A brass bird cage filled with geraniums. The flowers died, but Minnie kept the cage hanging in a corner there in the house.

A beautiful handmade flannel nightgown that Minnie wrapped in newspaper and stored away to wear in the event she had to go to the hospital.

A fish tank. She didn't like fish, but kept it full of water because it had one of them little deep sea divers in it, and she said she loved to watch them tiny bubbles a drifting to the top of the tank.

A re-winding clock that Minnie put up on the wall and remarked every time it whirred to wind itself, "Lord, if that ain't the lonesomest sound I ever heard."

And, one pretty summer Sunday, Howard brought Minnie a pedigreed dog, with real papers and everything. Keep in mind now that the only full-blooded dogs in Sodom at this time were hound dogs. Everything else was called cur or worthless, and usually both. But this was a real German Police dog. One that looked just like Rin-Tin-Tin on the

TV. The word spread quick in Sodom, and all of us went to see.

When all us young'uns got there, the yard was standing full of men, women, and young'uns. Some had come to see the dog, others had seen the crowd in the yard as they were going home from church and figured somebody had died, and others were just there.

But there was a good-sized crowd. Cindy was running back and forth trying to figure out how to feed this unexpected crew. Minnie was standing on the porch with her arm braced against the porch rail and her mouth full of Barton's snuff. Howard was standing in the dirt yard holding the dog by a fancy leather leash.

The dog was very noble looking, and he did look like Rin-Tin-Tin. Folks were standing back admiring him and commenting:

"Why, he is right purty, ain't he? Even if he ain't a hound!"

"They used them dawgs over in Germany to kill people with during the war. They would just say 'Sic-em-and-kill,' and them dawgs was so ferce they'd run and jump up on ye and rip your throat right offen yore neck."

The crowd moved back a little.

"Aw-w, what er ye a talkin' about? Rin-Tin-Tin ain't ferce. I hear tell they are about as smart as most folks. And they's supposed to be real fine and gentle and loyal."

The crowd moved closer again.

"And, he's got papers and everything."

"He shore has got purty eyes."

"Why would you look how his ears stand right up. Looks kind of like he's a prayin', don't it?"

"Ain't they part wolf?"

The crowd moves back a little farther this time.

And then Howard steps around in front of this beautiful creature and says sharply, "King, sit!" and the dog sits, watching Howard closely. "King, lay down!" and the dog lays down. "King, SPEAK!" And to our utter amazement, the dog barks two sharp barks!

"Why, ain't that dawg just absolutely somethin' to behold!"

Minnie had been watching all this commotion from the porch with a right scornful expression. She hadn't said a word. Cindy was scurrying back and forth passing out cups of cold buttermilk.

The young'uns had eased up to the dog and were petting him, marveling as to how bristly his coat was, how you couldn't feel his ribs a sticking out.

"Why, are you a gonna leave him here all the time, Howard?" someone asked.

"Yeah," he answered. "I've brung him to give to Mama. She needs a good dawg to sort of look about her."

The crowd nodded.

"Now, Mama, he has papers. He ain't like a regular dawg. You have to treat him special. He has to be fed bought dawg feed. He won't eat a bite a table scraps now."

This brings an "Oh-h-h" from the crowd.

"Imagine that now. A dawg that won't eat just anything. Ain't that just somethin'?"

Minnie steps over closer to the porch rail and lets loose a long stream of brown spit. She tongues her snuff back down in her lip and looks close at the dog. She studies him a minute, and the crowd grows quiet.

She sort of huffed and turned to walk back down the porch and then stopped, turned to walk back. She leaned down over the rail a bit and peered even closer at the dog. Howard, still holding the leash, looked at Minnie and said, "You hear what I'm sayin' to ye, Mama?"

Minnie looked at Howard and raised her eyebrows.

Howard said again, "He won't eat table scraps, just bought feed."

Minnie sort of sighed and said, "Ah, he'll come of it."

And he did, too. I swear that dog come to where he would eat anything, even raw cabbage.

Howard eventually came and took him back after a while. Everyone allowed as to how it was indeed for the best. And, to my knowledge, Howard never brought Minnie anything else that had to be fed.

Waterfalls and Rainbows

Granny told me when I was about six years old that every day I was with her she would provide me with waterfalls and rainbows. Now, I was old enough to know that the only waterfalls were a way back up in the mountains where the little streams came up out of the ground and made their way down until they rolled off over a drop in the ground and spilled out over the side of the mountain. I also knew that rainbows could be seen only when "the devil was a beatin' his wife." Mountain folks said the moment when the sun broke through the clouds, even though it was still raining, was when the devil was beating his wife. I wondered how Gran was going to manage this feat. I knew in my heart that Granny could do anything, so I knew she'd hold good her promise.

Granny always rose every morning at 4:30 and cooked one of the big breakfasts she was famous for: cat's head biscuits, thick, brown gravy, homegrown sausage and bacon, apple butter and fresh jelly blessed by Granny's hands, oatmeal, butter adorned with Granny's own leaf print from her wooden butter mold, coffee so strong that it could've stood on the table without a cup, and fresh milk. One bright spring morning I was helping Granny wash the breakfast dishes.

"Make sure that water on the stove is good and hot, Sealy," Granny said.

I peeped over at the near-to-boiling water in the pot. "It's ready, Gran."

She stepped to the stove and carefully picked up the pot and moved it to the table, where all the dishes were neatly stacked and ready for washing. She poured in enough water to cover the dishes in the dishpan and put the rest back on the wood stove to keep it hot for the rinsing.

After the dishes were clean and dried she looked down

at me and said, "Now, you go set down on the bottom step outside the kitchen door. I'll make you that waterfall and the rainbow I promised ye."

I settled myself and looked expectantly up at Gran. "Don't look at me. Face forward and watch," she said.

I turned dutifully and stared straight ahead. The chickens had gathered at the foot of the steps like they always did in hopes of scooping up possible tidbits out of the dishwater.

"All right, here it comes!" And with that I heard a great whossshing sound and felt droplets of water hit my head as Granny dashed the water over my head and out into the yard.

And there it was! I felt myself to be underneath a waterfall! And as the water flew past my gaze, there was the rainbow!

As the chickens scattered to avoid getting wet, I stood and danced on the steps. "I saw it Granny, I saw the rainbow!"

Granny laughed out loud and made herself busy wiping out the dishpan with her drying rag. "Yeah, I know you did. Come on in the house and we'll finish puttin' up breakfast."

I went in and sat at the table, marveling at Granny's abilities. She was over at the big white cupboard wiping down the pull-out counter when I noticed the paperbag.

"What's in the bag, Gran?" I asked.

She reached in and brought out a can. "This here is some blue spray paint," she said as she shook the can. There was the nicest rattle on the inside. I reached for it and Granny pulled it back into her body.

"Now, don't you touch this here can. I mean it." And with that she placed it high on the top of the cupboard. "This ain't no toy."

She turned and left the kitchen, going about the business of making beds and straightening up. I sat there looking way up at that can of paint. I listened to Granny singing softly to herself back in the bedroom. "That can sure did make a fine sounding rattle," I thought to myself.

Next thing I knew, the can was in my hand, and I was sitting at the corner of the house, shaking that ole can, listening to what sounded like a marble clanging around on the inside. I was beginning to get bored because I had already examined the can and had determined that there was absolutely no way to get that marble out; I was even thinking about slipping the can back on top of the cupboard, when Snowfluffy came around the side of the house and rubbed up around my legs. Snowfluffy was Granny's pride and joy. She was a solid white, long-haired cat and had one green eye and one blue.

She wound her way back and forth through my legs, purring to beat the band, not realizing the grave danger she was in at the moment. I looked at Snowfluffy and then at the can I held in my hand.

About five minutes later I looked at that cat and thought, "What have I done?"

Metallic blue paint had created raccoon stripes on Snowfluffy's tail! Her ears were blue. Her feet dripped with blue paint as she tentatively took each step, held out a blue paw and shook it. She had two racing stripes down each side, and I tell you, that blue stood out like you wouldn't believe against that snow-white fur.

It didn't take much thought to realize I needed to put that paint back real quick and find something else to do and somewhere else to be.

I was very busy sweeping the porch a little later when Granny came out, sat down in her chair there at the corner of the porch, put in a dip of snuff, and leaned back with a contented sigh.

"Look at my fine, clever girl a sweepin' the porch for her Granny. You sure are a doin' a good job. Granny really appreciates the help, and maybe later on we'll . . ." her words of praise trailed off, and she sat up straight in her chair. I picked up the pace of my sweeping and never looked around. I had a sinking feeling in my stomach because I suspected the fruits of my morning labors had made a grand and unwanted appearance.

"What in the world has happened to Snowfluffy?" Granny exploded.

I picked up the pace of my sweeping even more. "I reckon after I finish I'll go and git the eggs from the barn. Maybe ought to git 'em right now." With that I tossed down the broom and headed for the steps.

"Sealy!" Granny roared. "Look at that cat! What have you done to her?" By this time I had taken the steps two at a time and had almost cleared the yard.

"I don't know, but it sure weren't me that painted her!"

"You stop right where you are, and I mean it!" Granny shouted.

I stopped and stood there, my eyes exploring the ground at my feet like I had found something very valuable.

"Did you git that paint when I told you not to?" Granny asked my back.

Well, I figured if Granny was asking questions as to the guilty party then there might yet be some hope of getting out of this.

I turned hopefully, a lie forming in my head, and faced the porch where Granny stood. The look on her usually smiling face dashed any hopes of escape.

Snowfluffy was in Granny's arms, nestled against her clean, white apron–covered bosom. From where I stood I could see the blue paint soiling said white apron. I lowered my eyes to the ground and moved a scurrying ant along even faster with my bare toe. I found myself wishing I was that ant.

"I got the paint down just to rattle that marble and I took it out behind the house and was just a fixin' to put it back when old Snowfluffy come and I don't know what . . ." I looked at Granny and still no smile of forgiveness.

"Didn't I tell you not to bother that paint?"

A very reluctant nod.

"Go out yonder to the end of the yard and break me a switch."

My eyes grew big and round and I felt my mouth start to quiver. Granny was sending me, her darling, out to the switch bush! No, this couldn't be! I had watched grandchildren make their way slowly out to that particular bush before and had always felt smug and safe from my perch on the porch railing. I knew what always followed a trip to the switch bush. And now it was happening to me!

I also knew that when Granny called on one to make that journey it would be done – and quickly – or her wrath would only increase.

I plodded along and stood facing the bush, trying to remember advice from my cousins.

"Don't pick one that is too skinny and short. She'll throw it away and go get one herself and that's always much worse when she does it herself."

"You better not get one that's big and thick (as if I would anyway). If you do the whuppin' will go on forever!"

"Don't dare git one of the long keen ones. They cut the blood out of your bare legs."

All this information whirled around in my darting brain as I stood there staring at the bush before me.

I finally just reached in and broke off a limb – just a normal sized limb – and turned and took the longest walk ever back to the porch.

Well, the cat lived, I survived the one and only whipping Granny ever gave me, and now I have an aversion to even the smell of spray paint, especially metallic blue spray paint.

But Granny continued to provide me with waterfalls and rainbows for years to come. The last time was shortly after my daughter Melanie turned four years old. The two of us sat on the bottom step and watched as Granny whosssshed the water over our heads. Melanie laughed and danced on the bottom step in much the same way I had all those years ago.

As I walked through the kitchen door I looked at Granny and grinned.

"So, you got some spray paint that Mel can take outside and rattle?"

"Nope, I don't. But they's a broom out on the porch and hit shore does need sweepin'!"

Come See the Kittens

There was always a new batch of kittens around the house when I was growing up. I spent hours out in the garage playing with them, putting them in my doll carriages, dressing them in little shirts that Mama helped me make for them, and in general, tormenting them.

One summer our cat had blessed our household with eight of the prettiest kittens you had ever seen. I would go out early in the morning and play with them until Mama would make me leave them alone. I was always looking for ways to sneak back. I found a good reason one bright, white-hot morning.

Every summer, the local electric company came to Sodom and went around trimming trees and brush away from the power lines. They usually used what we called "chain-gang labor." I remember sitting at the edge of the yard and watching these tired looking men swing their axes and scythes. There was always a guard standing close by with a very big gun, so I never felt the slightest bit afraid.

On this particular morning, I had been threatened with a whipping if I went back out and bothered the kittens. So I was sitting on the porch watching the men as they worked down next to the road that ran by the house. I soon got bored with that and sat watching a wasp busy making a nest in a corner of the porch roof. The next thing I knew, there stood a man with a bucket in his hands.

"Howdy," I said.

"Howdy, to you too," he answered.

I looked out from under the shade of the porch at him standing there in the sun and decided right off that here stood my excuse to get at them kittens again.

"We got some new kittens. You want to see 'em?" I asked as I stood and walked to the edge of the porch.

"Why, I can't think of nothing I'd like to do more than see your kittens."

With that, I stepped off the porch, and he set his bucket on the ground. I reached out and took his hand in mine and led him around the side of the house and into the garage. He followed me to the back of the garage, where the old mama cat lay suckling her babies. I reached in and one by one placed them into his huge hands, where they all but disappeared. He fussed and praised each one and gently placed them back into the box with the mama cat.

"You must like kittens, don't you?" I asked as I looked up into his face.

He smiled and put that huge hand on my head, "I reckon I do. It's just been a long time since I'd held one in my hands. You must be awful proud to have such purty kittens to play with ever' day."

"Oh yeah, I am. But Mama says if I keep on wallering them that they're gonna git sick and die. All I want to do is hold them. That oughten to kill them. She told me a while ago that she was gonna whup me if I bothered them again. But I figured you would want to see 'em and all, so I brung you out here."

We looked at them some more, and he told me about a cat he used to have that wouldn't have anything to do with anybody but him. Wouldn't even eat unless he was the one to feed it.

I looked over in the box resentfully at my cat. "I wish I had a cat that loved me that much. This old mama cat will eat anything anybody gives her."

He looked down at me and smiled. "That might be good. That way at least if you was gone and couldn't feed it, at least it wouldn't starve to death."

I thought about this and decided he was probably right.

He patted my head again and said, "Well, I best git my water and git back. They'll wonder what happened to me."

I took his hand, and we walked back to where he'd left his bucket.

"You a wantin' water?" I asked my new friend.

"Yeah, that's what I come to git. But I sure am glad you showed me them kittens." he said.

I opened the door and stood waiting for him to come in. He stood hesitantly, holding his bucket. "Well are you a comin' or not. The water's in the kitchen."

He came up the steps, and I led him back through the house, where he filled up his bucket. I got him a clean glass and he talked about how good the water tasted. "My goodness, that surely is some sweet tastin' water."

I wondered about that. That was the first time I had ever heard anyone say water tasted any way a'tall.

He picked his bucket up, I grabbed his hand, and we made our way back into the living room. We were standing right in the middle of the room when Mama came from the back of the house and stood staring at us. I recall her face as it shifted and changed as conflicting emotions raced across her features. Now, armed with adult hindsight, I'm certain my mother was a little more than slightly taken aback by the sight of her seven-year-old daughter in her living room holding the hand of a very large black man who wore the gray uniform of a convict laborer, right down to the numbers on his shirt pocket.

"Mama," I said. "This is my new friend. He come to git water, and I took him out and showed him the kittens."

My friend set his bucket down and pulled off his hat. "I apologize for coming into the house, Mam. But this young lady invited me in and said the water was in the kitchen. And, I really wanted to see them kittens."

I must admit that old mountain charm surfaced nicely as Mama smiled and said, "Well, I'll be glad to show you where the outside water spigot is in case you need to get more."

She led the way out the door and around the side of the house where the spigot was, and he thanked her, thanked me again for showing him the kittens, and started off down the yard toward the road. I ran after him and took his hand.

"My name's Sheila. What's your name?" I asked.

"Mine's Chuck." he said.

When we got to the end of the yard he turned and smiled down at me. "You take good care of them kittens, now."

"Well, I reckon I will. I sure will, if I don't kill 'em first!"

Breaddaddy and the Furriner

I spent a lot of time with Breaddaddy during the summer months. I was what he called "easy company," and he was a lonely old man since Ma had died. Often was the bright and sunny morning that you would find me and Breaddaddy slowly making our way down the road, hands clasped behind our backs (me in perfect imitation of him), heads bowed, eyes on the gravel road at our feet.

He said I had more questions than rocks in the road.

"Why's the sky blue? Why are clouds white? Why can't I eat dirt, worms do? Why do weeds grow faster than corn? Why does Granny say God lives on top of Walnut Mountain? How come a cow will stand still and let a milk snake milk her? Do witches really come at night and saddle folks up and ride 'em all night? Why does Granny gather up fingernail and toenail cuttings and burn them? Is they really Indians buried in the Indian Graveyard?" And on and on and on.

He would answer every question without any sign of impatience. Where Mama would eventually throw up both hands and say, "Lord, honey, you just wear people out. Go play," Breaddaddy would take his time answering, slowly moving his chew of Beechwood Chewing Tobacco from one side of his mouth to the other, letting fly a brown stream of tobacco juice that made a satisfying "splat" sound and a small cloud of dust there on the road. Most of the questions he could answer.

Granny burned the fingernail and toenail cuttings to prevent witches from getting them and using them to cast an evil spell.

Dirt had worm and bug eggs in it and they would get down in your stomach and intestines, and then you had to take worm medicine. (I filed that bit of information away so I would definitely remember it. Mama had "wormed" me once and I didn't ever want to go through that ordeal again!)

There must be Indians buried in the Indian Graveyard 'cause it had been there since his grandfather could remember.

But if there was a question he couldn't answer he'd say,

"Well, now, I can't really say fer sure. We'll have to study on that one fer a bit. We might even have your Mam look it up in the Blue Books of her'n."

My questions and his answers would continue until we reached the store, which was located right in the middle of Sodom.

The store was a one-room building that sold pretty much everything we needed there in Sodom. But its main purpose was a gathering place where folks met up to socialize.

One fine summer day, Breaddaddy and I arrived and he bought me a soft drink (we called it a dope back then) there, and we wandered out to sit on the porch with Hitch, Roy, and Joe Don. I squatted down in the fine dirt next to the porch and was playing with the roly-poly bugs that were busy burrowing into the dirt. The men were saying they'd be glad to have their tobacco crop in the ground for one more year.

About that time we heard a screen door slam, and all heads turned to look up the road to the house where "the furriners" had moved in a few weeks before.

The furriners were from somewhere up north. The woman's name was Marta, and she had three girls. Word was, she was a widder woman, and it was a mystery to us how she'd ever found Sodom. But there she was, standing on the porch, drying her hands on a dishrag and looking out down toward the store.

The men fell silent and we all just sort of looked. Then she sort of flapped her dish rag at us and yelled,

"YOO-O-OH-O-O! Have any of you folks seen my Cooder?"

Silence for just a thought there on the porch. Breaddaddy first looked at me, then at the rest of the men on the porch. His face had a right bewildered, confused look on it, and he said, "Why, who in the world would want to?"

And the men on the porch exploded into laughter.

I was still right puzzled. I couldn't figure out why she would ask such a question. Especially to a crowd of men and in front of me! A mere child!

Anyway, she slapped that dish rag down, wheeled around, jerked open the door, and disappeared into the house.

When me and Breaddaddy were walking back up the hill toward home, I said, "Why Breaddaddy, reckon what made that woman ask us that?"

And he took a while to answer as the crickets chirped busily in the tall grass by the side of the road.

"Why, honey, I don't rightly know, but this is one that we won't find in them Blue Books of your Mam's. Sometimes they's questions that are best just left with nary a answer . . ."

Now, I found out later that Marta's middle daughter was also named Marta and was called Cooder. If Marta Sr. (or Marta Jr., for that matter) had known that the mountain meaning of that word described certain parts of the female anatomy, I reckon they would've found another nickname. But we were far too polite to tell either one of them.

The Mysterious Language of the Lord

hen I was about eight or nine years old, I remember Sunday mornings starting out at the Church of the Little Flower, where we'd all sit in on Mass, which was said in Latin. And when it came time for us to respond, why all us little young'uns with our pure mountain accents, would say exactly what we were supposed to say, in Latin. Now, we knew pretty much what was going on, we just didn't understand a word of what was being said. When Father Andrews was finished with Mass and was done blessing the congregation, us young'uns hit the door and headed straight for the Baptist Church across the creek, where we poured down the aisle and filled up that front pew.

Now, this was around 1960 and none of the roads in Sodom were paved. And there were dozens of us young'uns that had come down across the creek and up the road. We always managed to carry in with us the top layer of dust off the road. After we'd finally settled down, it took another full minute for the dust to find it a place.

Rosey Hunter, our piano player, would have just finished, "Are Ye Washed in the Blood?" and our dear preacher would rise from behind the pulpit where he'd been sitting. Manassey Fender looked like a pencil with a burr haircut, in a suit. He was about six feet, three inches tall and weighed about 130 pounds. He was prone to going to bed with his hair wet and apparently was a sound sleeper, because it looked as though he'd laid on the same side the whole night through. He was totally devoted to us, his scruffy flock, though, and he was a warm and gentle soul.

Every Sunday morning, right before the sermon, he would come over to where us young'uns were sitting to "speak directly to the little children," as he always said. Our heads would hit the back of the pew as we looked way above us into his face. And then he would say something like this . . .

"Phuffer fhe lipple childeun not buf bib 'um come unto mef, fer I anf th' way and 'th lipe. Now todaf, Preacher wanfs to tal to ya apout lyinf. Preacher knowsf tha' ever' oncet in a while lipple young'uns is tempeted to lief but when lipple young'uns liefs, whf all the angels in heavenf just breaks downf and criesf."

About this time little Robbie Lee would poke his sister in the ribs and say, "Sissy, what's he a sayin'?"

Because, you see, Manassey didn't have a tooth in his head, and although we would nod our heads solemnly while he was talking, it was just like Father Andrews and his Latin – we had no earthly idea what he was saying. We all grew up thinking that religion was one of the great mysteries of life that we mere mortals weren't supposed to understand.

It was when I was twelve years old that Manassey decided to retire from the pulpit. The preacher that replaced him had a mouth full of shiny white teeth. I could understand every word he said. It was also about this time that the Catholics decided to say Mass in English. I just figured that there had been a worldwide decision to speak so all could know. Amen!

Little Corrie and Otis

Little Corrie lived down the road from where I grew up in a huge log house that we called the Miss Fedrick's House. Miss Fedrick was sent here by the Presbyterians as a missionary, and my great-uncle Tim Metcalf built the house for her. In its time it was a lovely house. It was two stories tall and had hardwood floors. After Miss Fedrick vacated, it got the reputation of being haunted. My cousin owns it now.

Anyway, Little Corrie weighed about seventy-eight pounds sopping wet and was about four feet, eleven inches tall. She was also extremely nearsighted and would get up real close to you and peer into your face when she talked to you. This habit was a bit unnerving to us children, and we eventually decided that anybody that strange was probably a witchy woman.

Little Corrie was married to Otis. And bless his heart, he must've weighed 300 pounds if he weighed anything at all. He had been sick all winter and was older than God's dog anyway, and up in the spring of that year, he took a turn for the worse and died.

There in Sodom, we had about every flavor of Baptist you could imagine. We had Missionary Baptist, Freewill Baptist, Primitive Baptist, Southern Baptist, and plain old Baptist. Now, the Baptist church Little Corrie and Otis belonged to had gotten into a big row, and half the congregation had split off, left, and formed a new church. The ones who had stayed decided to buy Otis a new suit to be buried in. The other half were not about to be outdone, so they bought him a suit, too. So there was Otis, never having owned a single suit his whole life, with two suits to be buried in. So Little Corrie sent Otis, along with his green suit, to the funeral home, and they dressed him and fetched him home and set him up there in the living room.

The first person to show up that afternoon for the wake

was Little Corrie's sister, Clemmie. Clemmie made reference as to how his hair didn't look natural and requested a comb and brush and redid his hair, and they stepped back to look some more. Then Little Corrie, after looking him over full-length, said, "Why, you know, Clemmie, a lookin' at him a layin' there I believe he 'uld look better in his blue suit."

And Clemmie agreed with her. So, they commenced to changing Otis's clothes.

Little Corrie first tried crawling over in the coffin with Otis. She unbuttoned buttons and pulled and tugged, but Otis fit pretty snug in that coffin. She climbed back over the side, and they decided that the best way to get at him was to drag him out and lay him on the floor. Well, they tugged and pulled and managed to get him up on the side of the narrow edge of that coffin, and he fell on into the floor. Then they commenced to changing his clothes.

Little Corrie instructed Clemmie to lift his shoulders up a bit. Clemmie huffed and puffed and managed to lift him an inch or so off the floor. Little Corrie slid his suit jacket off and Clemmie eased him back onto the floor. Then Little Corrie allowed as to how she was going to have to have some serious help removing his trousers. Clemmie sat down facing Otis's huge tree trunk–sized legs and wiped the sweat from her brow. "I reckon the thing fer us to do is try to ease his britches down an' under his hips and slide 'em off both legs at one time. He ain't the easiest thing to work with, you know, all stiff like he is."

Little Corrie and Clemmie managed to get his pants off after much tugging and hauling at his legs. They slid the other pants up to his hips, then stood looking at him. "Well," said Clemmie. "Now, how would you reckon we're a gonna get 'em up over his hind end?"

Little Corrie took stock of the situation and said, "Well, we're a needin' to hurry. The way them britches is bunched up around the tops of his legs is a gonna wrinkle them things awful. And I just don't feel like ironin'!"

Clemmie grabbed Otis under one hip with her hands

and grunted. "Here. I've managed to lift him a bit. Slide 'em up an under him. Just do it quick. I ain't sure I can hold him long."

Little Corrie slid the pants up, and they repeated the procedure on the other side. Then they neatened him up and stood back to view Otis in his other suit.

And then it was time to put Otis back in his coffin.

By this time he had pretty much settled on the floor, and they couldn't budge him. They strained around until Clemmie said, "Lord have mercy, Little Corrie. I'm a gonna have to quit heavin' so hard 'er I'm a gonna bust a blood vessel. But, whatever are we a gonna do now? Folks is a fixin' to set into showin' up fer the wake, and he does look plumb un-natural a layin' there in the floor that a way. People'll talk."

Little Corrie stood wringing her hands, looking at Otis. "I know they'll talk. The only thing I know to do is to run up the road to Ervin's (Ervin is my Daddy) and git him to come down here and help us."

"Well, I reckon that's our only hope. You'd better git to movin'," Clemmie allowed.

So Little Corrie started off up the hill at a pretty good clip.

Now, my Daddy was probably one of the biggest New York Yankees fans that ever lived, and a baseball game was in progress on the TV. Daddy was totally engrossed in the game, and I was sitting on the couch watching Daddy, because sometimes it was a lot more fun to watch Daddy and listen to what he had to say than to watch the game itself.

The door to the living room all of a sudden flies open and hits the wall behind the door. And there stands Little Corrie breathing hard. It sounded like her asthma was acting up because she was wheezing bad. And she said, "Ervin, (breathe) you've got to come down t'th' house (breathe) and help me get Otis (breathe) back in his coffin."

Daddy turned glazed eyes to Little Corrie and said, "Why, where in the world is he? I thought he was dead."

And Little Corrie said, "Ervin, you fool, he is dead! Me

and Clemmie got him out'n his coffin to change his clothes, and we can't lift him to put him back."

And Daddy said, "Little Corrie, damned if you didn't worry him to death the whole time he was a livin', and you're still after him!"

But Daddy, being the curious and rascally type of person he is, stood up and started for the door. I stood up too. I wasn't about to miss this. Down the road we went to Little Corrie's.

We got there, went through the door, and there was Clemmie a standing right up over Otis, looking down at him. I don't know where she thought poor old Otis was going, but she was keeping a close watch on him.

Daddy and Little Corrie and Clemmie tried to lift Otis but they couldn't. They circled Otis like hawks for several minutes. They struggled and strained, but Otis didn't budge.

"Lord, Ervin," Little Corrie whined. "What are we a gonna do? It's a gittin' time fer folks to come and there he lays. Lord, Lord. What are we a gonna do?" And, with that, she took to pacing the floor.

Clemmie stood, looking to Daddy for an answer.

Daddy scratched his head and said, "Well, I can run down to the store. They'll be a crowd down there watchin' the ball game. I'll git some folks to come back up here and help me."

He left and was back shortly with a carload of men. With all of them helping, they managed to pick Otis up off the floor, shuffle over to the coffin, and sort of press Otis back down in it.

Then the men folk stepped back and started talking about the ball game and left me and Clemmie and Little Corrie there at the coffin. They kind of straightened him up and patted him down even further and looked at him some more. Clemmie fixed his hair.

And then Little Corrie stepped back, looked down the length of Otis, and said, "Why you know Clemmie, now that I look at him a layin' there, I believe I did like him better in his other suit!"

Briar's Baptism

On any given summer evening you could expect to find all us teenagers out at the "Chat Pile," with a big fire roaring and a hot game of post office raging. The Chat Pile was actually three small hills of stone used by the Department of Transportation to put on the dirt roads in Sodom. You might even find a gallon of moonshine being passed around or some beer being consumed in a furtive manner. All in all, we had a good time, and everyone enjoyed each other's company.

With the possible exception of Briar and Chester.

Briar and Chester were quite a bit older than the rest of us. Briar was in his late twenties and Chester was in his early thirties. They didn't have jobs outside the community. They both hired out to farmers there around Sodom, so money was usually pretty scarce with them. That lack of money was one of the reasons they hung around with us teenagers. As a group, we usually had some sort of alcoholic beverage that we had purchased from the local bootlegger, and Chester and Briar knew they could bum something to drink. Also, both of them smoked cigarettes, and in a crowd of that size, they figured they could stay supplied with smokes the entire evening. They were tolerated by all of us, mainly because, at times, they could be downright entertaining.

See, as the evening progressed, Chester and Briar would get roaring drunk. They would sing and tell stories and keep us all laughing long into the night.

That is, unless it turned out to be one of those evenings that Chester got religion. When he got the spirit, he always focused on poor old Briar.

Briar was a slim fellow with just the beginnings of a beer belly. His face was always flushed and covered with a thin sheen of sweat. He had a red, bulbous nose, little black eyes that sat pretty close together beneath his mono-brow, and fat little cheeks. His thick, curly black hair would have been his best feature if he had left it alone. But no, he wanted it to lay flat to his head, so he used Brillcream – by the handfuls – trying to get it to lay down. So, his hair always had a dull-looking, greasy film.

As I said, sometimes Chester would get religion on these hazy, warm, sweet-breezed summer nights and start to preach in the old-fashioned Baptist way. He would spring to his feet all of a sudden and start to dancing around the fire screaming a string of Glory Hal – a – lu – years, Blessed Jesuses, and Amens. And the rest of us would lean back and wait. We knew what was coming. Briar would start to rouse a bit from his drunken mutterings and look real worried. He knew what was coming, too.

Chester would jump and twirl for sometimes ten or fifteen minutes. His shirt would be wringing wet, and the sweat would be streaming off his nose. His eyes would get a fanatical gleam to them, and he would fall upon his knees and shudder and begin to pray for all us sinners. He prayed long and hard and sometimes would even talk in "tongues." If anyone dared to move, Chester's eyes would snap open, and he would point his finger and say, "Dare you ignore the word of the Lamb?"

Usually, the person who had moved kept on about their business, and Chester went back to his praying – unless that person was Briar. Chester did not want Briar to move; he wanted him to listen and be "saved." Actually, Chester zeroed in on Briar whether he moved or not. But if he dared to try and slip off while Chester was praying, things happened at a much faster rate.

Chester would lunge across the space separating him from Briar and grab him around the neck. Briar would flop around feebly, but Chester would usually manage to wrestle him down. And then the praying would resume, although now Chester would be praying specifically for Briar to "come clean, name your sins." And Briar always refused to cooperate – at least at first. Chester would not be swayed from his mission. The praying and crying and shouting would go on for hours, or at least until Briar realized he was going to have to give in before Chester would let him get up. Usually, Briar would relent and say he was ready to pray with him, and they would pray awhile, then both would go back to their drinking.

It was during the dusky-dark time right before night falls on Midsummer's Eve that Chester decided to do things right where Briar was concerned.

It had been a hot, clear day and most of us had gone swimming in the creek after supper. We congregated at the Chat Pile and were sitting outside our cars beneath the trees that hung out over the mounds of rock, cloaking them in cool, deep shade. Music from the car radios drifted lazily out of the open windows, seeming to float on the heavy, still air. Nobody was up dancing; it was too hot. Robbie had his beach umbrella planted on the very top of the largest of the chat piles and was stretched out in his lawn chair almost asleep. It was from this vantage point that he roused himself, shaded his eyes, and called out, "I see Chester and Briar a comin' round the curve over yonder. If you got any beer left, you might want to hide it."

There was a scramble below as folks grabbed their few remaining beers and stowed them in the trunks of their cars or stashed them underneath the seats. Cigarettes were flung into glove compartments, where they were locked up tight. Then we all resumed positions and waited.

Chester and Briar had just finished up working on a new barn old man Rice was raising, and they were hot and sunburned. After checking out whether anyone had any beer, they came up dry and decided to visit the bootlegger themselves. They left and were back in a bit with three six-packs of tall ones. They commenced to drinking, and before the sun had set good, they were getting right. By the time the sky had begun to darken in the west, and the big old full moon was rising in the east, the Spirit was on Chester good, and he zeroed in on Briar with a religious zeal unlike any we had witnessed before.

Briar was laughing and telling some big story when the first "Glory Halaluyear" split the hot, humid air. Chester danced and screamed in such a manner that he could've put our former preacher, Manassey Fender, to shame. He flew into hard, on-his-knees prayer almost immediately. I glanced over at Briar, who had stopped midsentence and was looking at Chester with a wary watchfulness. He started to ease off to the side, trying to get a car between him and the wildly gesticulating Chester. He was actually able to take several unsteady steps before Chester's eyes grew wide and round and nailed him to the spot. Chester opened his mouth, screamed like a wildcat, and lunged at Briar. He wrestled him to the ground and got him in a tight headlock.

"Briar, I'm a prayin' for the salvation of your soul. I'm a tryin' to keep your pore soul from roastin' eternally in a hot bed of coals. Are ye with me, Briar?" Chester hollered.

Briar muttered something unintelligible.

"Speak up, man. Tell these people what you're a feelin' in your heart." Chester said in a softer, but just as intense, tone of voice.

Briar managed to get his mouth high enough off the ground to whine, "I said you're a breakin' my arm!"

"Yes, there is pain that we have to feel in order to make our way clear through to them pearly gates. Talk to me Briar, do you feel the Lord's presence yet?"

"Hell no. I just feel these here rocks a stickin' in my belly. Git off'en me Chester. Let me git up now," Briar said, as he began to struggle in earnest.

Chester held Briar with one hand and raised the other high in the air. He was crying for real now. "Forgive this pore miserable sinner, Lord. Come into his heart so that he may know You and come to love You."

Chester, sobbing loudly, brought both hands up and clasped them in prayer, and it was then that Briar made his move.

He gave a mighty heave and began to squirm out from under Chester's legs. They thrashed about for a few min-

utes with Chester preaching and Briar cussing. They finally rolled over to the edge of the mountain, where it gently
sloped down to the creek below.

Hank yelled, "Somebody better grab 'em! They're a
goin' over!"

The folks closest jumped and ran. But we were too late.

With a final mighty heave, Briar toppled Chester over
the side. Chester, realizing he was gone, grabbed Briar, and
the two of them disappeared into the darkness.

We all stood anxiously around the top and listened as
they crashed around down in the dense undergrowth there
on the mountainside. Then there was silence. We figured
as how they were probably dead or at least seriously hurt,
and some of the older boys had started down to carry out
the bodies, when there came a tremendous splash from the
creek.

We all tumbled over the side then, sliding and slipping,
grabbing hold of trees. At the bottom we all piled out onto
the rock that jutted out over the creek. There was Chester
holding Briar waist deep in the creek. Both seemed un-
hurt, but Briar seemed unsteady. At least it seemed he was
leaning awful heavily on Chester.

Then Chester's voice rang out clear and strong, "Briar, I
baptize you in the name of the Father, the Son, and the
Holy Ghost."

He lowered Briar until he was totally immersed.

As Chester brought Briar back up to the surface and
helped him to stand, beating him on the back while he
gagged and sputtered, Briar finally gained his voice and
said "Now, Chester, that's done. Will you leave me the hell
alone?"

Anything to Save a Soul

During the winter, the Chat Pile at Peach Tree was abandoned to the cold wind and snow, and us teenagers would congregate at the little one-room store there in the middle of Sodom. Since the older folks had to go to work the next morning, we'd find ourselves left to our own devices. Which was fine with us. We'd play the jukebox and dance to songs like "I'm So Lonesome, I Could Die," "Wipeout," and "Woolly-Bully." There was also a pool table and a couple of constantly tilting pinball machines. There was always a great deal of grab-fanny foolishness going on. Robbie would fly into imitating one of Sodom's many characters, or we'd decide to play "Who you're with, where you're at, and what you're doing." Whatever we were doing, you could bet there was always much shared laughter and enjoyment of each other's company.

It had become obvious to Chester (and everyone else) that Briar's baptism hadn't took back in the summer, so Chester decided to set Briar right once and for all.

One cold, snowy winter night we'd been dancing and drinking beer. Briar was laying stretched out on the pool table almost asleep. The door opens and in steps Chester. Snow had collected on his head and shoulders. He had his hand on the doorknob, holding the door open while snow and the cold wind whistled in. Things got quiet when we all saw that he was looking at Briar with that certain look in his eyes. With a great flourish he slammed the door. He pointed a finger at Briar and said softly, "Repent, pore sinner, repent."

Briar sat bolt upright and whipped his head around in Chester's direction. A look of pure, unadulterated fear crossed his face. "Now Chester – don't you go a startin' that ole stuff. I ain't a botherin' a single soul."

Then Chester did a shuffling little dance out into the

middle of the room. Briar was watching him from his pool-table perch like a hawk.

"It's time to get right, Briar. Hit's fer yore own good now. You know it is." Chester's voice had dropped to almost a whisper now. I reckon he realized his prey was a fixing to fly if he didn't use a gentle hand.

Briar, while keeping a wary eye on Chester, kind of scuttled sideways, putting as much green felt between him and Chester as he could. Chester started easing over to the table, talking low and kind of soothing-like. Briar managed to slip over the side and gain his feet. They stood facing each other with the pool table between them.

We figured we'd just let this growing drama work its own self out. We all settled back to watch.

Chester broke to run around the table, and Briar took off. They must've run around that table twenty times. All you could hear was grunting and mumbling. When they were both pretty much out of breath and hanging onto opposite sides of the table, Chester said, "Now Briar, ain't they some sane way we can settle this without either one of us getting hurt?"

Briar was not a fool. And he was kind of tired. A right crafty expression settled on his face. "There might be some way, I reckon. But now just how fer are you willin' to go?"

And Chester, smelling Briar's possible salvation, says, "As fer as I need to Briar. I'll do anythin' to save yer soul."

And Briar, with a bit of gleam in his bloodshot eyes, says, "Anything?"

And Chester throws his arms out and shouts, "ANYTHING!"

And Briar says, "OK. Suck eggs."

Well, you could've heard a pin drop in that store.

Chester, with a puzzled look on his face, says, "Come again?"

And Briar says again, "Suck eggs."

He crossed his arms over his chest and looked smug.

"Suck eggs?" Chester asked.

"Suck eggs," Briar stated.

And with that, he walked to the refrigerator and opened it, reached in, and brought out a dozen eggs. He carried them over and set them down on the pool table in front of Chester. He opened up the cardboard crate and looked at Chester.

"You said anything. I want you to suck all twelve eggs down. If you can do it, then I'll work with you. But only if you can do it. If you can't, well, then you've got to leave me alone."

Chester looked at them raw eggs, then at Briar. Without another word he reached out and picked one up.

We watched as Chester ate the first three – all the while with Briar looking on with a right satisfied, clever expression. By the sixth egg, we were all cheering Chester on, even though, judging by his greenish tinge, we didn't think he could manage to do it. When he downed the ninth one, Briar's expression had started to change, and his face had begun to pale. Chester managed just fine, and when he held up the twelfth and final egg, he looked at Briar with a look of expectation. Cracking it on the edge of the pool table, he turned it up and drank it down without so much as a flinch. He crushed the shell in his fist and raised it over his head. We all applauded loudly.

When things had quieted down and Chester had been slapped several times on the back and duly congratulated, all eyes turned to Briar.

With nothing but a sigh of resignation, Briar sank to his knees. Chester knelt, real easy-like so as not to jar them eggs too much, placed his right hand on Briar's head, and began to pray.

To my knowledge, Chester never bothered Briar again after that. Briar's habits didn't change much, but Chester did admit later that he never had cared much for eggs, and he cared for them even less now.

Bertha and the Snake Handlers

Churchgoing was always a moving experience in the community of Sodom, especially revivals that were held out under a big tent in the summertime. These revivals offered some entertainment value as well as an excuse to socialize. And they broke up the monotony we young folks experienced through the long, hot days of any given summer. The singing was wonderful and sometimes would go on late into the night.

But there was one church experience that "moved" more folks than any other in the history of Sodom. That was the summer the snake handlers came to the High Ridge Church up on Little Mountain.

As soon as I heard they were coming I headed for Bertha Franklin's. I found her sitting on her porch. Bertha was a rare find – a big, stout woman who would sit telling her stories or singing her love songs in a strong, rich voice for hours. She used her hands to punctuate her stories and songs to the point where she once said that if somebody sneaked up on her and cut them off she'd just be mute for the rest of her days. She laughed from deep in her belly, slapping her knees, her eyes shining. She could be downright imposing whenever she chose. She was also one of those people that had no filter between her brain and her mouth; what she thought came straight out her mouth. I figured if I could talk her into going to this event, there would be stories to tell for years.

"Bertha! Guess what's happening at the High Ridge Church this Saturday night?" I said, plumb out of breath from all the excitement.

"I already heard what foolishness is a fixin' to take place up there, and folks what would go to somethin' like that is foolish, er bored, er both!" she exclaimed hotly.

"Now, Bertha," I said. "Ain't you the least bit interested

in what them folks do in one of them services? Not even just a little bit curious?"

"Lord, no," she fired back at me. "Why would I be curious about a bunch of damn fools carryin' on with snakes and fallin' down on the floor and frothin' at the mouth? I got enough to do watchin' these fools runnin' up and down the road out there ever' day. I don't have to go lookin' fer idiots and fools. They somehow manage to find me!"

We ended the conversation right there. At least for that day.

I was back the next day, though, begging and pleading for her to go. And the day after that. I spent the rest of that week trying to talk her into going. Finally, on Friday, she agreed to go.

"You git yourself down here early now," she said. "You recall how long hit takes me to git in and out'n a damn car."

I pulled into her driveway a full hour before the service was to start. There she was waiting for me on the porch, all dressed up for church, her good pocketbook gripped underneath her arm.

"I had about give you up fer comin'," she hollered as I came up through the yard.

"Why now Bertha, I told you I'd be here early to git you. We've got plenty of time."

"Well, hit depends on whose definiton of early you're a goin' by, now don't it?" she said as she came down the steps, placing her feet carefully on the rickety boards that sagged with her weight.

When we got down to the car, Bertha began her usual procedure that she practiced whenever she had to ride somewhere.

She opened the door, turned, and backed up until the backs of her legs collided with the frame. Then, she eased down till her fanny made contact with the seat. Next, she took her two hands and placed them securely around her left leg and lifted it into the car. Then, she reached back out and lifted her right leg in. She raised herself slightly and tugged her dress out from under her person, reached back out, and slammed the door hard enough to rock the car on its frame.

"It is just too damn hot to wear this big ole heavy dress. I sweat so hit's just a stickin' to me like my own skin. I'm sure to burn up in that infernal church. Hit'll be hot enough to bake bread on the pulpit up on the side of that mountain," she quarreled as we moved off up the road toward the church.

And it's a good thing we went early. It seemed a bunch of folks had decided to receive the word that night.

"Now, Bertha," I said as we entered the door of the church. "We've got our choice of seats, and we might want to sit here at the back, close to the door, so we can git out in a hurry if we need to."

Bertha turned and looked at me from where she stood in the middle of the aisle, a slight smile curling her lip. "No sir. I have come to see this durn show, and I'm a goin' right down to the front bench so's I'll have a good viewin' seat!"

And with that, she sailed on down the aisle and seated herself on the very first bench. As we settled ourselves, she started to look around.

"Where do you reckon they've got them snakes?" she said as she nodded to someone in one of the back rows. "Why, I want you to look! There's Jake Gosnell and, why, over there's Buck. Now, Lord if that ain't a sight to behold! Them two hellions inside a church!" She laughed big and loud and poked me in the ribs.

The church continued to fill up behind us, and there was much talking and movement as people tried to find a seat. Eventually, all seats were taken, and people started standing around the walls and spilling out onto the porch and even into the dirt parking lot in front of the church.

I can remember the sounds: the rustle of hymn books that were being used as fans, young'uns fussing and being told to hush, the hum of chatteracks outside the open, screenless windows, the low talking of the people in the yard, an occasional cough from someone in the congregation, and Bertha's breathing, which had begun to sound

[75]

like she was huffing. She was getting more and more agitated as time went on.

"I don't see one single soul that would have the nerve to handle no snakes. I bet you this was some sort of deal to git folks like me inside a church! I'll not stand fer none of that tryin' to save me, now. I'll just not put up with these fine folks a gatherin' round me a prayin' and carryin' on. They'll be trouble if they zero in on me!" All this was said as she looked me straight in the eye, her lips stretched over her teeth in a sneer.

"I don't think you have a thing to worry about, Bertha." I answered aloud. To myself I thought, "No ma'am. Nobody in their right mind would mess with you looking the way you do right now. Not if they value their life!"

About the time I was thinking I was going to have to leave and take Bertha home, six people entered the church from a side door and stood there kind of huddled together. Two of the men placed large wooden boxes right inside the door.

"I bet them's the snake handlers. I ain't never seen them before. And I bet them's the snakes in them wooden boxes," she announced triumphantly. "Let's git this show on the road!"

A man in light green polyester pants and a pale yellow shirt, buttoned all the way to the top button, separated himself from the small group of strangers and walked out into the middle of the floor there at the front of the church. The entire crowd quieted down immediately, and all that could be heard was Bertha's quick, raspy breathing. The man said "Let us pray," and proceeded to lead a lengthy prayer filled with many a "Yes, Lord" and "Hep him, Jesus."

When the last amen had been uttered, Bertha looked over at me and asked out loud, "Well? When are they a gonna git out the snakes?"

I assured her I didn't have the faintest idea and patted her knee. But I knew we were entering a different stage of difficulty when she crossed her arms over her mighty bosom and a look of defiance slid over her face. She began to bounce her leg up and down, and the whole bench started shaking.

"Is there anybody here this evenin' that would like to stand up and testify afore I start my sermon?" the preacher asked.

Directly behind Bertha a woman stood slowly.

"I got somethin' I need to git off'en my heart," the woman said softly.

"Bless ye, sister. You go right ahead," the preacher said. "We're all here fer the same reason."

Bertha snorted big and loud. I patted her knee again.

"I been a member a this here church since I was a little girl, and if you ask me, most folks are here fer the wrong reasons. Iffen you'll look up there at the little wooden plaque a hangin' to the left a the pulpit, you'll see there was just twelve people here last Sunday. Why, iffen you was to count all the folks inside and outside the church there must be close 400 here tonight! I think hit's a sin and abomination what's brought all these people here. Handlin' them snakes in church is a scandal! You ought to be ashamed a yourselves. Everyone of you. Especially you what has brought 'em in here. I say you ought not do it." The congregation was dead silent as she sat down.

Now, I don't know if they would've got the snakes out or not, but that woman's hind end had no more than hit that bench than that preacher made some kind of strange sound and every head whipped around to look. He set in to jerking all over.

Bertha, who had been glaring over her shoulder at the woman, snapped her attention back to the front and immediately uncrossed her arms and leaned forward. The preacher was hollering and preaching in what sounded like a foreign language. He looked like he was going to have a stroke any minute.

When he paused, Bertha said, "Yessir, they'll git the snakes out fer sure now. He's took to talkin' in tongues."

The preacher by this time was foaming at the mouth, and I for one was getting a bit concerned. Then he started shaking even harder and said something like, "She-e-e-e-ma-ma-ma."

Then he screamed just like a woman.

Bertha clapped her hands. "Yessir, that really stirred him up. Here we go!"

He lunged across the room to the wooden box and threw back the top. His hands disappeared into the box, and he brought out two of the biggest rattlesnakes I have ever seen – and they were in full sing. A gasp went through the crowd.

Bertha chose this moment to stand bolt upright, turn and face the congregation with outstretched arms, and holler out in her big, ballad-singing voice, "Why Hell! Them's REAL snakes!"

And the entire congregation exploded.

Everyone left however they could. Parents were throwing children out the windows to folks standing outside. People were screaming, praying, hollering. "Catch little Johnny," someone yelled, and I saw a little boy of about seven go flying out the window.

I looked toward the door and was amazed. Benches were turned over, and people were shoving and fighting, trying to get out the door, which looked to be hopelessly jammed.

Bertha looked back at the preacher, who was charging around with those two big snakes held at arm's length, and said, "Girl, I'm a thinkin' that hit's time fer us to be a gittin' out a here!"

From my position up on the bench where I had climbed after the snakes appeared, I pointed at the door and screamed so as to be heard, "We can't get out, Bertha, the door's blocked and, honey, *you* can't git out one of them windows."

She looked behind her one more time and saw a woman had joined the man and was running back and forth with two copperheads.

With eyes rolling and a look that resembled, for all the world, a startled horse, she yelled at me, "You grab a hold of the back of my dress, girl, and I'll show you how we'll git out of here!"

Well, I grabbed hold of her, and Bertha went down that aisle like a ship in full sail. As I said, Bertha was a big woman. She shoved and pushed and hollered and cussed her way out of there and told such awful secrets on anyone that dared to block her path that I'm sure they haven't recovered to this day. We wound up being one of the first ones in the parking lot.

Bertha was stepping mighty high off the ground, and when I asked why, she said, "They might've turned some of them serpents loose on the outside to test our faith like they was a fixin' to do on the inside!"

I started stepping high too.

We reached the car, and I started around to the driver's side. I hadn't any more than cleared the back bumper when Bertha was in that car with the door closed. There was none of the usual posturing and positioning herself. I mean, she launched herself into that car and slammed the door in one fluid motion!

Bertha didn't say a word on the ride home. I kept glancing over at her expecting her to start cussing me at any minute. I was a nervous wreck by the time we pulled into her driveway. She opened the car door and began her usual process for getting out of a car. She lifted her right leg out and placed her foot on the ground, then her left leg. Then she braced her arms on either side of the door to heave herself out. She looked back at me and said in a very soft voice.

"Now, honey, I think the world of you. Why, you're just like one of my own. You're welcome to come down here and sit on my porch and I'll sing them old love songs all night long and never sing the same one twice. But don't you ever, ever, ask me to do something like this never again."

And I said meekly, "Yes Ma'am."

And I never did.

Whatever Happened to John Parrish's Boy

Hearing the old songs was as much a part of my growing up years as waking up in the morning. Granny was one of those that was always singing. She sang while she worked, "Young Emily was a pretty fair maid, she loved the driver boy. He drove in the main for some gold to gain way down in the lowlands low." The high lonesome sound of Granny's song would drift into the still air and fade. She sang "Young Emily" while she milked the cow. I would stand, feeling the warmth of the cow next to my side as I held onto that tail for dear life. See, it was my job to hold the cow's tail while Granny milked. Otherwise, especially during the spring and summer, that tail would come out of nowhere and slap Granny in the head. So I was the official tail-holder for many a milking.

I never thought the old songs where all that valuable. I just knew that Granny sang of Lords and Ladies and Spirits and Sprites (and you could tell just by the tone of voice she used that they were capitalized). And she always sang with more strength when she was outside. See, anything inside the house was considered work – outside everything was fun!

We spent a lot of time together, me and Granny. She used to say, "My hand print is all over the raising of that one." She cleaned many a stubbed toe and scraped shin while I was growing up. And looking back, I appreciate the many times she scooped me up in those strong arms that knew so much about loving and holding. As I grew older, my interests shifted a bit. Now, I was a child of the sixties and listened to the radio just like other folks my age. But Granny, without even meaning to, kept me firmly planted in Sodom.

Out of all the people Granny knew that had a driver's license, I was the only one she considered her step-and-fetch-it. She would call up and order me up to her house to haul the ballad singers to some backwoods community center or some basement in some little church so far off the road that you had to drive as far as you could, then get out and walk a mile. These gatherings were called Round-Robins. The room would usually be empty except for a huge circle of chairs in the middle of the room. The time would usually be around seven o'clock in the evening. Granny always liked to be early for these events, so we would usually sit around waiting for thirty minutes or so before anyone else showed up. But sure as rain, folks would start to come in, and slowly the chairs would fill. A little before seven o'clock, every single chair would be occupied by an ancient (ancient to me then meant over forty) male or female; and before long the room would swell with the sounds of the old love songs as one after the other of these singers took their turn. I attended many a Round-Robin.

Driving to these events was a real trip, in more ways than one. The crew, as Granny referred to us, usually consisted of me, Granny, and Berzilla up front, and Inez, Cas, and Vergie in the back. Inez was of a considerable size, and since Cas and Vergie were small, they got to ride in the backseat with her. Cas used to say that he'd ridden on Inez's hip enough to where he felt like he ought to be one of her young'uns. We'd load up, and off we'd go.

We had many an interesting conversation riding back and forth. Vergie liked to talk, and she usually did – non-stop – all the way there and back. Cas usually wanted to sing me a song, so he would lean up on the back of the seat, right next to my ear (right ear for a regular old love song; left ear for a dirty one) and sing nonstop all the way there and back. Granny and Berzilla were normally pretty quiet, and Inez kept up a running conversation with me about everything and anything that happened to dart through her mind.

One evening, we were en route to Warren Wilson College, and as we headed up the Marshall Mountain, Granny interrupted Cas, who was singing right low into my right ear. She also managed to bring a lull to the conversation between Vergie and Inez, who were talking fast and furious across Cas's back.

"Lord that was awful about John Parrish's boy, weren't it?" Granny asked mournfully.

For a moment there was silence in the car. "Who?" asked Cas.

Inez screamed into Cas's ear, "John Parrish's boy, I believe she said."

Vergie said, "I don't believe Buck Parrish had a boy. Him and Lou only had girls. Let's see. They was Joan and Margie and Susan and Rosie that I recall; but I don't believe they had a single boy. Me and Margie was born within a month of each other, and I remember the time she cut her foot while we was a wadin' in the creek. They had to take her off to the doctor in Marshall, and we all thought that was the biggest thing 'cause folks didn't go off to the doctor like they do nowadays. You know, I was a tellin' Cas just the other day that I am amazed how folks run off to the doctor at the drop of a hat. Why, we just couldn't do that all the time for ever' little thing that happened to us or ever'time we got sick. Why, Lump fell one time and come near to bustin' his brains out, and he never went nowhere near a doctor. I'm afraid of 'em myself. They ain't no tellin' what them doctor's will put you on, and the last time I went I saw pore old Patty there, and you know she ain't no better now than she was."

Berzilla interrupts here and says, "You mean Patty's boy? What happened to him?"

"No, not Patty's and Weston's boy," Granny answers. "I'm talking about John Parrish's boy."

Silence in the car. "Who?" asks Cas again as he briefly removes himself yet again from my right ear.

Inez leans over and screams into Cas's ear, "Jake Parrish's boy, I believe she said."

"No," says Vergie. "I really don't think Jake and Ev had any boys either. Now wait a minute. Now that I think of it, they might have had one boy. Sim, I believe he was named.

You know, they named him after Big Sim Gosnell. 'Course I always thought that was funny 'cause Sim weren't his real name. Seems like hit was Arthur or something like that. Now, that was who Sheila's uncle Arthur was named fer. Er maybe they named him ater Bob's great-uncle Arthur. Why, you know, I bet that was the way hit was, 'cause why would they a named Arthur ater Sim Gosnell, 'cause he weren't that close a kin to Bob ner Emily neither. Lord, I remember when Arthur was born. Hit was in September of 1920 . . ."

Inez interrupts with, "Arthur? Sheila, honey, nothing's happened to Arthur, has it?"

Before I have a chance to answer, Granny says, "No, not to my knowledge. I'm a talkin' about John Parrish's boy."

"Who?" asks Cas again.

Inez answers in an even louder scream, "She said something about Sim Gosling's boy, I believe."

"Well," Vergie says. "Now Sim and Gert DID have several boys. They named one of 'em ater Jimmy Norton. Now, he was fer a fact Big Bob's brother. 'Course him and Sissy had a bunch of young'uns afore he died of typhoid. They lived right up there at the foot of the Sim Mountain. Right down from where Dellie's house is now. They was a old log house used to set there before you started up the mountain itself, and I remember goin' there as a girl. Mom would stop and set on the porch with Sis, and they would talk. Molly used to come up there a lot too. Lord, I always loved Molly. She had somethin' wrong with her mouth and had trouble talkin', but seems to me like that after she married Wade hit got easier to understand her. Now, Molly was Emily's sister, weren't she? Why, yeah, I know she was. That was the purtiest place her and Wade had down there on the Wade Clift. They took good care of their place, and Molly always had the purtiest flowers. I used to go out of my way just to git to walk by the house so I could see the flowers . . ."

Berzilla interrupts with, "John Parrish didn't have no girls, did he?"

And Granny sighs and says, "I ain't talkin' about his girls, I'm talkin' about his boy, his boy."

"Who?" Cas asks.

"Now, Cletus did have a boy," Vergie says after a brief silence. "His name was Joe, and I remember when he was born. It was in 1928 and there was a big snow on the ground. They used to come the biggest snows back when we was growin' up. Why, the weather has changed like you can't believe just in the last ten years or so. I remember my mother talkin' about it snowin' to where you couldn't get out to the barn to feed for days. Said the snow would just swirl around your head to where you couldn't see a foot in front of you. Now, they had it rough back then . . ."

Inez interrupts with, "Dellie, what happened to Sim's boy?"

"I don't know nothing about Sim's boy, I was talkin' about John Parrish's boy."

"Who?" Cas asks, with the first hint of irritation in his voice.

"John Parrish's boy!" screams Inez.

We pulled up in front of the building on Warren Wilson Campus, and I jumped from the car to help my precious cargo disembark.

Berzilla sprang out and hurried through the door, followed by Vergie and Cas. Granny stood waiting with me as Inez struggled to free herself from the confines of the backseat of Mama's Monte Carlo.

As Inez straightened her clothes and gathered her pocketbook, and I got back in to move the car to the parking lot, I heard Inez ask Granny, "Well, what DID happen to John Parrish's boy, Dellie?"

And Granny very wearily answered, "Hell, he died."

Off to Ivydale

·················

It was back during the early seventies when us young folks in Sodom suddenly realized that we might not have near the level of sophistication we had originally thought. Fresh out of a high school, which had graduated a whopping senior class of sixteen in 1970, we entered the Big World with freshly scrubbed cheeks and big ole grins, only to discover that we were somehow different.

Some of us went straight into jobs in Asheville or Johnson City, Tennessee. Some of us went on to college. I went on to Western Carolina University, where I was immediately forced to accept the fact that, somehow, I was just not like the majority of young adults that had come from all those heard and read about but as yet to be visited places like Orlando, Nashville, Wilmington, and Pittsburgh.

I felt as lost as one of the Tribes of Israel. My roommate was from Miami, and I made my first faux pas by pronouncing Miami with a short vowel "a" sound on the end. After the laughter subsided, my roommate asked me to say it again. So I did. After the second round of laughter, I figured I ought to just keep my mouth shut.

Four weeks later, Daddy was helping me load my belongings in the car for the trip home. A girl on crutches limped by and stopped to chat. When she got out of hearing distance, I said, "That's the one, Daddy."

He watched her struggle with the door to the dorm and said, "Why, she's right purty. Now why do you reckon she would launch herself out of a second story window the way she did?"

And I replied, "'Cause she said she could fly."

Daddy looked out across the parking lot, where students were moving to and from class, and said softly, "She thought she could fly? Well, don't that beat all?" And he laughed.

That was the end of my brief attempt at attending a big university. I returned to Sodom and started Mars Hill College in January.

It was during my years at Mars Hill that I began to venture away from the confines of the mountains around Sodom. It wasn't near the shock that Western Carolina offered because it was done in short spurts and I was just like a rabbit. I would dart out into an alien world and quickly retreat back to Sodom to sit on Granny's porch and dip snuff and drink homemade wine.

In the summer of 1972, four men from West Virginia showed up in Sodom to put on a music festival. They had received a grant from the Rockefeller Foundation to fund this endeavor, but how they found Sodom remains a mystery. Anyway, they put on the festival in June, and it was a great success. As they were packing up to leave they mentioned they were having a festival in Ivydale, West Virginia, in August and invited us to come. So me and four cousins began right then and there to lay our plans to go.

Since none of us had driven that far before, we figured we'd best leave early. So we struck out before daylight. One of the fellows from West Virginia had told us it was about a six- or seven-hour drive, so we assumed we'd roll into Ivydale around two o'clock that afternoon.

But, that was not to be.

We made great time till we hit the West Virginia line; then things started to get real interesting.

There were five of us, all about the same age, all having grown up in Sodom: Sharon, my first cousin, and I had slept in the same crib together and shared bottles. Besides us, there was Hank, who was attending the University of North Carolina at Asheville and was letting his hair grow; Fletch, who was learning to play the banjo; and Chuck Arnold, who was one of our cousins from the Ben Cove.

We spent a lot of time rubbernecking. We knew West Virginia was known for its coal mining, but we couldn't figure out what folks were doing cutting all them roads out around the sheer sides of the mountains. We did reckon as to how it looked pretty awful. We finally asked somebody at a gas station and got our first instruction on a mining practice called strip mining. We spent a while back on the road in silence and then Sharon said, "Eh, Lord, I'm glad they ain't no coal in Sodom."

After a while we realized that the road had a pretty steep grade to it and what had been a clear blue sky was full of giant thunderheads, especially around the top of the mountain we were climbing. Sharon remarked as to how it appeared we were driving straight up to Hell. We all laughed. But a few minutes later, we didn't think it was so funny.

The first fat raindrops hit the car about half the way up the mountain, and by the time we got to the gap, it was raining harder than any of us had ever seen. Chuck Arnold said this must be what old folks back home called a "frog-strangler." I was having trouble driving, so Hank suggested we pull over and wait out the storm at this gas station right at the top of the mountain.

An hour later, the storm was still going on and showed no sign of letting up. If anything, it had gotten worse. The rain was coming down in sheets, and you couldn't see beyond six feet. The lightning had struck twice out on the ridge, and the thunder coupled with the wind had given us quite a scare more than once. Hank decided that the storm was most likely stuck. Sharon turned around and told him to shut up. She reminded him that noise drew lightning. We finally figured we might as well go in the store and get some cigarettes and something to drink and be on our way. We all dashed from the car and ran into the store, and Sharon said, "Damned if it ain't raining so hard out there I actually breathed in water!"

We bought what we wanted and then all of us clustered around on the porch, dreading hitting that downpour again. Finally, Chuck Arnold remembered he needed to call home, so he ran for the phone booth and we ran for the car.

I pulled the car down next to the phone booth, and we waited with engine running and wipers flapping furiously at the steady assault of water. Hank peered through the window and said, "What in the Hell is taking him so long?"

About that time a blue ball of flame started bouncing around inside that metal phone booth, and Chuck Arnold jumped about three feet straight up and came flying backwards onto the pavement. Hank said, "Well, I'll be dipped in buttermilk. Looks like Chuck Arnold just got struck by lightning."

Chuck Arnold hit on both feet and lunged for the car, eyes and mouth wide open. He piled into the backseat, trembling and moaning. He looked around wildly at all of us. Every hair on his head was trying to repel the others. They were all standing straight out.

He said, "Is they smoke comin' out of my ears? It feels like they's smoke comin' out of my ears."

We assured him that it wasn't smoke, just his hair, and by the time we pulled out onto the road, he'd begun to calm down.

Halfway down the mountain, the rain began to let up and had just about stopped when we reached the bottom. We pulled in at another phone so Chuck Arnold could call again and let everyone know he was still alive.

It was here where Chuck Arnold discovered that he had lost his billfold, which contained all the money he had in this world and his driver's license.

We sat for a long time, looking back up that mountain.

We could tell by the play of the lightning in the clouds that the storm still raged. I looked over at Sharon and her mouth was drawn into a tight, pinched line. I felt Hank's hand give my shoulder a squeeze. Fletch sighed through his nose. There was nothing to do but start back up into the fog.

Halfway up, the rain hit again, and at the top, it was as if absolutely nothing had changed.

The parking lot was, by this time, running like a river. We drove slowly over to the phone booth, and I must admit I have to admire Chuck Arnold's courage. He had pulled his shirt off and had it wrapped about his head and had such a look of fright on his face that I almost didn't open the door. He must've read my expression because he said, "Open the door now while I can still force myself out of this car."

He hunched his shoulders, lowered his head, and disappeared into the storm.

He was gone a long time but finally appeared like a ghost on Hank's side of the car. He tapped on the window and Hank rolled it down just a crack. Chuck Arnold said, "I can't find it. Younse is gonna have to help me."

With no more than a quick glance at each other we all abandoned the relative safety of the car and stepped out into enough water to float a good-sized boat. It didn't seem as though the rain was falling down. It appeared to be coming at us sideways.

Fletch found the billfold. Right behind the phone booth was a metal pipe that drained the water off the top of the mountain and shot it straight out over the side, where it dropped halfway down the mountain before it touched earth again. Anyway, Chuck Arnold's billfold rested comfortably in the opening of the pipe, and Fletch just reached in and plucked it out.

There was much laughter in the car going back down. Whenever a car passed in the opposite lane, spraying us with a wall of water, we would howl and carry on about what lay in store for them at the top. Sharon lit a cigarette with shaky hands, and we teased her unmercifully.

"What's the matter, Sharon? You ain't nervous, are you?" Fletch chuckled.

"Hell no, not now I ain't. I'm just trying to get something in my lungs besides water!" she shot back.

We all screamed with laughter.

Soon, we were off the mountain and the sun came out. The air sparkled and shimmered. We had survived!

Chuck Arnold made his phone call and set everybody's mind at ease back home, and we struck out for Ivydale, now hoping we'd at least make it before dark.

Well, this was not to be either.

We did make it to Charleston before dark. But we discovered the directions given to us didn't work. The Department of Transportation had been real busy in Charleston; it seemed the road we were supposed to take had just disappeared. We must've spent three hours driving around on the back streets of the city. We finally decided we might ought to stop and ask at a service station. We stopped at one we had driven by several times and asked. The man behind the counter smiled, pushed his hat back on his head, and said, "Why yeah, I can tell you how to get to Ivydale. My brother's wife's from Ivydale."

Armed with directions and renewed hope, we struck out.

Two hours later we were sitting beside a two foot by two foot sign that said IVYDALE. And that was all. Oh, there was a little store there too, but I assume since it was 1:30 A.M. that those good folks that ran the store had been asleep for several hours.

"Well, what now?" Hank asked.

No one even bothered to answer.

About thirty minutes later a car pulled in behind us. Sharon muttered, "Oh God, we're all going to die. They'll rape me and Sheila and throw us over the bank." She looked around at me and shuddered, "Nobody would ever even find us."

Hank said, "More likely, we're fixin' to get put in jail."

We all groaned.

A man climbed out of the car and walked up to the driver's side. I rolled down my window and to my disbelief sat looking into the grinning face of Briar!

"Why, if it ain't my ole cousins, Sheila and Sharon. And why, is that you Fletch, Hank? Why, and there's Chuck Arnold too!"

"Briar! What in the world are you doing? How'd you get here?" Sharon asked.

"Why, I was walkin' out of the holler to the store and Ernest Lewis stopped to give me a ride and said he was on his way to Ivydale, West Virginia, and I said I'd like to ride up with him if he didn't care, so here I am. And I was just wonderin', have any of younse got a cigarette I might could bum?"

I gave him a cigarette, and he leaned against the car smoking. He finished, thanked us, and turned to go back to the car saying, "Well, we'll see younse. Are younse a sittin' here for a perticular reason?" he asked.

"We figure to wait till mornin' and ask these folks that run the store where this music thing is," I answered wearily.

"Oh well, if you just want to wait on them, that's fine." Briar grinned. "But if'n you want to git on over there tonight, follow us. I know where it is."

Ten minutes later we were there.

A Ballad by a Different Name

I was nineteen years old when I walked into Dr. Harley Jolley's world history class at Mars Hill College. Even though it was located in Mars Hill, right here in Madison County, there were kids attending classes with me that were from all over the United States. I learned as much from these other kids as I did from any classroom situation.

I truly enjoyed Dr. Jolley. He was by far the best teacher in an academic setting I had ever had, and I learned things about the world that really set me to thinking, really broadened my viewpoint. But in this particular incidence, my own limited experience was brought into the bright light of day.

I rushed to Dr. Jolley's class one lovely fall morning. We were just beginning the study of the migration of the settlers from the British Isles. I couldn't wait to hear what wonderful facts and stories he had to share about my people. Why had they come here? What kind of people were they? And on and on and on.

As we settled down for the class, Dr. Jolley stood in his usual place at the front of the room. He was always dramatic. I waited with held breath.

"Well, folks, we start today on a fantastic journey of one of the largest and diverse mass movements ever noted by historians. I speak, of course, of the migration of people from the British Isles to America. They came by the thousands – they came wealthy and poor, educated and illiterate, upstanding members of the community and society's outcasts. They came searching for freedom or a place where they could establish communities that enabled them to practice their particular brand of intolerance. Whatever their reasons, they came, and they came in droves, by the thousands they came, bringing with them their customs, their traditions, their heritage. The strengths of that heritage have been preserved, passed down through the generations, and there is no better example of this, especially in the isolated coves and hollows right here in the mountains of Western North Carolina, than the music."

I perked right up at this bit of information.

"We have right here in this classroom a person who has been the recipient of this strong practice of these settlers, a keeper of the old songs."

I sat up even straighter in my chair and looked around trying to identify this person, knowing that I would definitely want to talk to them after class, pick their brain, find out what songs they knew, where they were from.

"And what better way to introduce a culture than to have a person from the culture share what is near and dear to them. So, Sheila I am going to ask you to share with us one of the old songs."

My head whipped around and I sat staring at Dr. Jolley.

The room was quiet. I could hear more fortunate students walking and talking and laughing outside the open windows. I could hear the girl behind me breathing. I quickly shot a prayer toward heaven, "Open up floor, please."

All eyes turned toward where I sat. My eyes were glued on Dr. Jolley's figure at the front of the room, where he stood, eyebrows raised forming a question mark on his forehead.

I was mortified. But, I was also not above brownnosing. I stood and cleared my throat and began making my way up the aisle.

Dr. Jolley smiled. I faced my executioners (the class), and then Dr. Jolley said, "And class, we're in for a real treat! Sheila does a cappella!"

My mind whirled frantically. "Acappella, Acappella, Acappella?"

I looked at Dr. Jolley and finally said, "Well, these old love songs are known by a lot of different names, and if you could talk out the first line of this Acappella or at least tell me how the story goes, I might very well know it by another name."

My vocabulary increased that day, at least one word.

Cherry Goes to a Party

. . . .

My friend Cherry came from Charlotte. She had grown up there and then had gone off to Greenville, North Carolina, to the university there. So, she was pretty much a city girl. But I didn't let it bother me, and she was a dancer with the Old-Time Cloggers, so we became fast friends. I invited her home to Sodom with me for Thanksgiving one year, and she wanted to meet Granny, so she came.

Of course, word of her upcoming visit spread quick, and we got all kinds of invitations to parties and gatherings. One gathering in particular was talked about for years – the party where Cherry met Grover.

It was cold that Friday night after Thanksgiving. The sky was so clear that the stars looked like little chips of ice tossed out on a piece of black velvet. Cherry and I had been invited out to a gathering in West Asheville, where we'd been promised that there would be plenty of music and that these folks "really knows how to set a good table" and so we decided to go.

It was at Belle Ann's son's home, and she insisted that we "just had to come go with them." And we did, along with her two grandsons, her daughter-in-law Wilma, and Grover, one of her other sons. We were a bit crowded in the car, but Belle Ann said we'd be OK since we were only going into Asheville, a mere hour and ten minutes away. It did get a mite close in there, but the two boys kept rolling the windows up and down and up and down, so at times you actually felt as though you were out under all them stars. Wilma drove like a maniac, and we had to hold on for dear life. Belle Ann sang while Grover talked. And Cherry pretty much kept her mouth shut, which was unusual for her, especially for that long.

Eventually we got there, and one of the boys received a

resounding slap somewhere about the head for stepping in Granny's lap. I heard Cherry give a shuddering sigh because, after all, she had majored in child psychology at East Carolina.

The house, in a subdivision, was a huge brick split-level with every light on inside and all the floodlights on outside. Belle commented on how it appeared that they "was a practicin' for the sun to rise." The drive was lined with cars. We could hear bluegrass music being played inside the house.

When we got to the front door, Cherry was in front. As she reached for the doorbell, Wilma pushed her and said, "Law, don't knock, honey. We's family!"

We all followed her in and were met by a plump woman with platinum hair wearing a lime-green polyester pantsuit. Keep in mind that this was in the early seventies and most everyone that Cherry and I associated with wore jeans and cotton shirts – which is exactly how we were dressed at the time.

The lady of the house smiled and took us into the kitchen, where there must've been thirty women and men standing around eating southern fried chicken and drinking "sodey-dopes." All the women had on polyester pantsuits, and the men had on knit pants and pullover velour tops.

Belle Ann kept telling me to play my banjo, which I'm always happy to do. Old-time banjos cannot compete with bluegrass, though, which was going strong in the next room. Finally, though, the bluegrassers took a break and wandered into the kitchen. I got my banjo and went into the living room and sat down on the couch. Cherry was sticking pretty close to me, and by this point she had a strange, wild expression on her face as she looked around the room – kind of like she might bolt and run at any minute. I scanned the room, looking for something that might have spooked her, but all I saw was a nice enough room decorated with solid wood furniture. I figured she just felt out of place, so I reckoned the best thing to do was to get her to dancing.

I started playing "Rockingham Cindy," and Belle Ann set in for Cherry to dance. Cherry looked around wildly at the carpet. It would prove hard to dance on all that wool. Belle Ann pointed to the tiny brick area right in front of the door leading outside. It was about three feet by three feet, but Cherry is a good sport, so she went over and started to dance.

While the bluegrassers were still in the kitchen feasting on chicken, Belle Ann's son Grover came in to the living room. He had his big Gibson banjo in his hand and sat down beside me and started to play with me – very loud and totally out of time. I finally just had to quit, and he took that as a sign that it was his turn to solo.

He ran through five or six tunes at a blistering pace and ended each song with a resounding BRANG-G-G. Cherry had stopped dancing by this time and had wandered over and sat down in the chair facing Grover across the table in front of the couch. He sensed a captive audience now and really started to put on a show. And he started to sing and to sweat.

After the first three songs, Cherry began to sag down in the chair and massage her temples. She nevertheless kept her eyes on Grover and a smile fixed on her face. She was, after all, raised polite.

All of a sudden, Grover stops mid-BRANG-G-G, reaches up, jerks his hair off, and tosses it on the table. Then he reaches in his mouth and removes both upper and lower plates and throws them on top of the wig. "This here wig is a burnin' me up, and them teeth is a killin' my gums! Now I'm shet of 'em!" he hollered.

He must've had an eyelash in his eye or something because his fingers started plucking at his eyelid. Cherry screamed, "No! You stop right there until I leave this room!"

She gained her feet and literally bolted in the direction of the front door, leaving me and Grover looking at each other, right puzzled-like.

"Wonder what struck her?" Grover asked.

I told him I didn't know, but I'd go see.

I found Cherry huddled on the top step of the porch. She looked perfectly green. I sat down beside her and asked what was wrong.

She looked around at me and said, "I didn't know he was wearing a wig, so that startled me. The teeth coming out and being laid on top of the hair was a bit strange. But damned if I'm going to sit and watch someone pluck out their glass eye! That's just absolutely too much!"

Nellie's Trip to D.C.

In 1976, the folks up in Washington, D.C., fanned out across the nation to round up "real" people who were carrying on the old traditions or maintaining their heritage. Us people in Sodom had pretty much been ignored (which was fine with us) by the government for 150 years, so imagine our surprise when these two folklorists showed up telling us about this big festival that was going to take place up in Washington on the Fourth of July. They wanted us all to come and sing the old ballads and tell our stories. They said they'd pay for everything and give us money to boot. And we would get to fly up there! I found myself in the position of expert because I was the only one that had any experience at flying: I had flown to Philadelphia once. You would have thought the older folks would be a little hesitant, but they weren't in the least bit worried.

As a matter of fact, they were so excited they couldn't sleep for a week.

We had to go to Raleigh first to perform at the State Folklife Festival. We all drove down there and were to catch the plane out of Raleigh/Durham Airport for D.C.

We rode to the airport before daylight. Nellie, who was seventy-eight at the time, and Leona, who would be eighty-four in just a few weeks, chattered like young girls.

"Nellie, did you think to bring them hairpins? I swear I don't know where I lost mine. Why, I believe I'd lose my very head if the good Lord hadn't seen fit to screw it tight to my neck."

"Leona, are you sure Dan'll go milk fer me? I told Jake, too, but that boy ain't got no memory a'tall sometimes."

They were both as giddy and giggly as young'uns. I started to relax. I had worried to start with. See, they depended on me an awful lot. They figured I had been out in the world more and knew how to manage. But I knew the truth. I was as much a big-eyed gal at the fair as they were. So I had been worried, but now I figured things would go just fine.

When we got to the airport, we were herded to our loading gate, where they piled all our carry-on stuff onto the belt to be X-rayed. Leona was in front of me, and Nellie behind. I handed Leona her pocketbook after it came through the machine and turned to get mine. That was about the time the alarm started whooping. Nellie grabbed her pocketbook off the belt and popped it under her arm. The little slip of a girl behind the machine was looking at Nellie with huge eyes, and it was all so confusing that it took me a minute to remember what Nellie never left her house without, and what she never left home without usually had all six chambers loaded.

I gave an inward groan and said, "Nellie, something you've got in your pocketbook is a causin' all this commotion." I was trying very hard not to say the word out loud.

Nellie looked right puzzled for a minute and then her face lit up. She took her pocketbook out from under her arm and said, "Why, Sealy, I ain't got nothin' in here 'cept this . . ."

Before I could get to her to stop her, she reached in and pulled out a snub nosed .38 with all chambers loaded!

The young girl reached instinctively for the gun, and Nellie held on to her end. So they pulled back and forth across the conveyer belt for what seemed like a right smart amount of time – or at least they struggled until five security guards had converged on the scene. I can only imagine the picture we painted for them: Leona standing, hands on her hips, shaking her gray-bunned head saying, "I told her to leave that miserable thing at home, but she never would listen to nothing I told her, not even when she was little, always determined to do just what she wanted to. Well, I guess she'll learn to listen ever' oncet in a while now . . ."; me with my hand over Nellie's, looking on the outside every bit as wild as I felt on the inside; the tiny black girl behind the belt hanging onto the wrong end of a gun; and

Nellie, a big, rawboned mountain woman with a look of determination on her wrinkled face.

I finally screamed into Nellie's ear, "Let 'er go or they'll put you in jail, and the rest of us'll get on that plane and go to Washington without you!"

She let go so quick that the girl holding onto the other end almost dropped it and fell back a step or two.

After everybody had calmed down and quit breathing so hard, I explained that Nellie certainly meant no harm, and of course they could bag it up and put it somewhere else; and finally we were allowed to move on toward the plane.

There was a woman from Florida along with us who played the banjo. I guess she figured the whole ordeal must've surely tired Nellie out, so she had a hold of her arm, leading her down the aisle of the plane toward her seat. All of a sudden, Nellie jerked her arm away from Anne and charged down the aisle, pushing Leona to the side and flinging herself into the seat.

Anne hurried to Nellie and said, "Miss Nellie, Miss Nellie, are you OK?"

Nellie looked up with a smug expression and said, "I had to hurry. I knew Leona was a headin' fer the window seat and I meant to have it!"

Anne said later that she had learned not to take them two old gals at face value.

And I responded with, "You got that right."

I went back to their seats once during the flight to make sure they were OK, and there they were, both with a face pressed to the window. Leona reached over and took hold of Nellie's hand, and I heard Nellie whisper, "Now ain't that just something, Leona? Have you ever in your life seen anything to beat this?"

I didn't interrupt them. I turned quietly and made my way back to my seat.

In the Works

There were eight of us that went to the Bicentennial Festival in Washington, D.C. We stayed in a Georgetown University dormitory and were shuttled back and forth to the festival every day. Nellie never got used to the way the drivers would weave and jerk through traffic. She alternated between prayers and curses the whole trip there and back. When we weren't at the festival she sat at the window in her room and took aim with the by now infamous pistol at every plane that roared by the entire week. She'd say, "Click! Yessir, I got me another'n, Leona."

And Leona would say, "Just think of all them folks a fillin' up all them planes. Why they take off day and night 'bout ever twenty minutes or so. Where do you reckon they all go?"

Nellie would snort and say, "Well, they're all a helluva lot smarter than us! At least they got enough sense to leave this place!"

Leona would respond with, "Oh shut up. Honey, you quarrel all the time."

The very first night we were there, I made sure everybody was settled in for the night and that they knew where my room was, then I fell exhausted into bed. Later, I heard this scratching/knocking sound on my door. I hauled myself up, and when I fumbled around and finally found my glasses and looked at the clock, it read 2:35. I went to the door with a heavy heart wondering, "What NOW?"

When I opened the door, there stood Leona, dressed in her long white night gown, looking for all the world like a little white bird.

I felt my heart gentle as it always did at the sight of Leona.

"What's wrong, honey?"

"Oh, nothing's really wrong. I hated to bother you, but

I was wonderin' if you knowed where the bathroom might be?" she said barely above a whisper.

I pointed to the closed door across the hallway and told her I'd go with her. She was washing her hands when she apologized again for bothering me. I assured her there was no apology needed. Her little arms reached up and hugged me, and then she said, "Anyhow, I feel right foolish. Why, all along, the bathroom was right here within spittin' distance and I've been wanderin' around down in the works for what must've been close to an hour a lookin' fer it."

"Down in the works?" I repeated.

And she nodded sweetly, "You know, downstairs in the works, where they have the furnace and everything. I figured that's where they's bound to have the bathrooms."

I said, "You mean down in the basement?"

She said, "Yeah, that's what I said, down in the works."

Answers to Life's Questions

I had to face the idea that Granny was not going to live forever one beautiful summer day in August. I had gone to Sodom early and gathered corn for canning with Daddy and was back home with one pressure canner on the stove ready to come off and one ready to go on when the call came.

My cousin Sara's voice wobbled and lurched as she told me that Granny had just been taken to the hospital. They were afraid she'd had a massive stroke and weren't sure she'd make it through the trip to Asheville. But before leaving the house, she had grabbed Sara's hand and said, "Sealy," as plain as day.

"She's already asked for you, now. I think you need to hurry," Sara said as she cried.

I had already turned off the stove by this time and told Sara I was on my way.

A thousand images crowded into my mind. The winter day Granny had made me two pairs of underdrawers out of a flour sack, and how bewildered I was when I discovered Mama had thrown one pair away. I hid the other pair and wore them only when I went to Granny's. The time me and Granny walked all the way to the Marshall Watershed and got caught in a thunderstorm and had to lay down in a cleared field so as not to get struck by lightning. And all those times on the porch as she patiently sang verse after verse of the old ballads and listened as I sang them back.

"No, now, Sealy, put your heart in it," she'd say. This here is a powerful song. You want hit to sound like you're a sufferin'."

So many memories.

I cried as I drove, praying for her to live just so I could see her one more time. It was then I realized how bound I was to this woman. I was as unprepared for her death now as I was when I was ten years old. She had been a part of my life since it began. She was the most exciting person I had ever known and the best teacher I would ever have. As she had often said,

"My hand print is all over the raising of this one."

Sara met me in the lobby of the hospital and said, "She's still alive. They've got her in the intensive care unit, and she's asked for you twice more. Says she's got something important to tell you."

As we rode up in the elevator I thought, "This is one of the most important hours of my life. I've got to try to remember what it feels like. Granny is fixing to tell me the answers to all my questions about life. That's why she's asking for me."

With hot tears burning my eyes and throat I went through the door of the little room where Granny lay, and for the first time in my life, I realized that I was bigger than Granny. She had always seemed so strong and huge to me. Laying there with IV needles stuck in her thin arms, I saw that she wasn't much bigger than my eight year old son.

I walked over to the bed, carrying this knowledge like a rock hung somewhere right beneath my heart. Her head was turned away from me, and I reached out, took her hand, careful of the needles, and whispered, "Gran, I'm here."

She turned her face toward me, and when my eyes met hers, my spirit leaped for joy because, judging by the clearness of her eyes, I knew she hadn't had a stroke.

She smiled and said, "They took my glasses. I can't see you too good, Sealy, honey. Lean in here a bit, I got to tell you somethin' real important."

I leaned down till I could feel her warm breath on my cheek and waited, my heart pounding, thinking, "Here it comes, here it comes!"

She looked me straight in the eyes and said, "Don't you *ever* cut your hair again."

And I responded after a moment of swirling thoughts, "Is that all?"

And she said, "That's all."

Well, Granny didn't die. She had a kidney infection that had caused blood poisoning. In three weeks she was back sitting on her porch cussing her guineas.

That was four years ago. My hair is below my waist now. I think somehow a deal has been struck between me and Granny. As long as my hair remains uncut, she'll keep living. If that's the case, then I wonder how I'll manage when it drags the floor?

Granny's Birthday

Granny turned ninety-three years old yesterday. And I made that same journey that I've been making for as long as I can remember. Most of the road has been paved now, but there's about a quarter of a mile that is exactly as my mind stored it as a child. The stream bounces and sings over to the left of the road, and the buckeye trees reach out to touch each other overhead, casting a cool shade in the summer. But this is fall, and buckeyes lose their leaves early on, so they're pretty much bare now.

There's always a crowd gathered to celebrate Granny's birth, each face as dear to me as one of Granny's old quilts, each person a square stitched together by the strong thread of her love. And the laughter! My cousins and I gather in the kitchen, and I get caught up again – just like always. I feel myself slipping easily back into the comfortable and familiar rhythms of my family. I'm home again.

There was a time when we talked of babies – we all had one then. Granny would move around, weaving between stretched out legs, smiling, talking, offering advice, like "Only thing I ever give mine for loose bowels was watered down blackberry juice. It'll tighten 'em right up"; or "When a young'un is six days old you've got to turn 'em up by the heels and shake 'em good. It keeps 'em from getting liver growed."

And every pair of mothers' eyes goes to one of their own. Granny laughs and says, "Oh, don't worry about none of Granny's young'uns. I shook ever one of 'em. Shook 'em good too."

A collective sigh of relief goes round the room.

Before babies, we talked of men and love.

"Love's one of them mysteries, I reckon. And them men. Lord, Lord. They are somethin' to try an' please, ain't they? I'll have 'em figured out one way and then they'll do right the opposite. So I've come to this way of thinkin'."

All eyes turn to Granny. We wait for her words of wisdom.

"I figure, if truth be known, THEY feel about the same way about us!"

Disappointment registers first, then a giggle starts, and soon we're all roaring with laughter, slapping our thighs. The men peep into the room, eyes round and curious, only to shake their heads and turn away. One of them mutters "Women!" which only makes us laugh that much harder.

And before that, there was talk of shaving our legs.

"If God had meant us to be slicker than glass, why He'd a made us that way!"

And talk of first periods and dolls and how best to shoot marbles, with a demonstration right there outside the kitchen door. And lessons on how to play set-back, Granny's favorite card game. But she never taught us how to cheat. Oh no, that was a secret known only by her and Delphie Gunter.

The talk this year turns to "the change of life." We're all of an age to start thinking toward menopause. We talk about who has had a hysterectomy. And there are some familiar faces that are no longer here – Marthie, Granny's daughter, died of cancer two years ago. I miss her. Marthie's daughter, Dean, is living in Florida and couldn't get off work to get here in time. Melanie, my daughter, has a big test tomorrow and can't get away from college.

There's even talk of grandchildren now. Jane has a granddaughter that she's raising. Dean has two grandchildren. While Jane talks, my eyes move around the room, touching each face gently, and finally lock with my cousin Sue's. Sue is sixteen days older than me, and her Ashley is two months younger than my Melanie. They'll be twenty years old soon. Sue smiles and nods at me. It won't be long before we're grandmothers. Time passes. I smile back and nod.

"We'll grandmother together, just like we've done everything else," I say. She crosses the room and puts her arms around me, and I rest my head back against her body. And for a moment my eyes blur with hot tears.

"Yes, we will," she says and rubs my head, smoothing back my hair.

The gathering starts to move into the other room, where Granny sits. Pictures are taken, hugs are shared, and then it's over. Someone says, "Well, I reckon we better go." I look at Granny. She looks tired. It's time to go.

As I bend to hold her, her arms go around my neck. I'm startled by her strength. She holds me a long time.

"I love you, Sealy. You're my own."

"I know Granny, I know. I love you too. You're one of my own, you old rubber-necked chicken. You're gonna live forever, I reckon."

She pulls back, arms locked around my neck.

"You always was the one with the smart mouth. Should've whupped the infernal Hell out'n you four times a day."

I laugh and bury my face in her shoulder, breathing in the smell of her.

And then I leave. From inside the house I hear her say to someone, "Well, I guess we'll do it again next year."

I hope so, Gran, I hope so.

October 4, 1991

Ending Granny's Story

On Tuesday, September 14, 1993, somewhere around two o'clock in the morning, my Granny, Dellie Chandler Norton, passed away. We were planning yet another birthday party. She died quietly and without too much of a fuss, just like she would've wanted it. She also died with dignity, at home where she wanted to be.

In April of this year, Granny buried her baby daughter, Mary. I went to be with Granny, and as we sat there, me on the couch, her in her chair, mere inches separating our knees, I looked into her face, so still and ravaged with her grief. I leaned across and touched her hand.

"I love you, Gran," I said.

She closed her hand over mine and smiled. "I know you do, Sealy. I know you do."

She turned her head slightly and gazed out the window. "I want you to promise me something, will ye?" Her eyes came back to rest on my face.

"If I can, Granny," I said, my eyes holding hers.

She studied me silently and I waited, my heart quiet.

"I want you to sing my song, that one you wrote fer me when I turned ninety, at my funeral," she said finally.

"Oh Lord, Granny, I don't know if I can do that or not. I don't know that I would be in any kind of shape to do that."

Her grip tightened on my hand, "Oh, you'll figure some way to manage it."

We sat frozen, my hand in hers for a long time.

"And I want you to stay for the whole thing, too," she said, eyes still holding mine.

"What do you mean, the whole thing?" I asked, my heart becoming heavy.

"I mean the whole thing, start to finish. I mean the whole thing." Her voice trailed off and she stared out the window again, eyes far away.

"I'll do it, Granny, I promise," I said softly to her.

She smiled and absently patted my hand. I sat there until I figured she had gone on to thinking of something else. I pulled my hand from hers and leaned back into the couch.

She focused back on me and said, "Of course you'll do it. They never was any doubt."

And I did. I sang "Granny's Song" at the end of her funeral service. I climbed the hill to the graveyard above the Catholic Church there in Sodom, and I sat as they laid her in the ground.

It was the hardest thing I have ever done.

It is hard to believe that someone who carried Daddy and Mama in her arms at their birth is no longer there. She also carried my sister and me and all our kids in those same arms. She told me stories, taught me songs, and gave me the gift of her memories about my family. Her life almost spanned a full century. She was one of the few left having been born in the 1800s.

She was my greatest teacher, my beloved grandmother, and my best friend. I will miss her for as long as I live.

Weather Breeder

Oh, there is so much to remember. Take the winter of 1961. It snowed pretty steady from December through February, and the drifts on the north side were pretty impressive. I remember Daddy taking me out and setting me down in a drift that was up to my armpits. I remember, too, feeling shivery and that it was hard to breathe.

And, Lord, it was COLD!

One night during that winter (and my memory recalls it as a wonderful winter) it started warming up during the evening, right before dark. The snow already on the ground started to melt, and I was so disappointed. Mama and Daddy talked of it being a "weather breeder."

I thought, "What in the world? How funny that sounds."

When I asked, Daddy said, "It's a warm spell in the winter that comes in on a breeze from the south. It usually starts with rain, and then the temperature drops quick, and it all freezes. Then it starts snowin'. It's usually a good one, too."

All the snow had just about melted by my bedtime, and a warm, springlike rain had started to fall. I hadn't been asleep long before the deep rumble of thunder woke me. I got out of bed and went into the living room, where Mama and Daddy stood looking out the window. I wedged myself between them as a lightning bolt snaked its way from heaven to earth and hit the ridge over at the Inez Garden.

"Well," Mama said, "I always heard the old folks say lightning in a winter night meant snow before daylight."

And Daddy swooped me up from the floor and said, "But just in case, Sealy better get to bed 'cause if the old folks miss on this one, they's gonna be school tomorrow!"

But the old folks didn't miss.

By midnight, pure ice was falling from the sky, and, by two o'clock, the biggest snow I can remember had started to fall.

It was still falling when Daddy woke me and told me to get dressed. The power line had gone down somewhere, and the house was freezing cold. We didn't have a wood-stove, so when the power went, our heat went too. So we were going to my Daddy's Aunt Flossie's house.

"But it ain't daylight yet," I said.

"It will be in a few hours," Daddy said. "We can't risk drivin' because of the ice on the roads. We're gonna walk it."

Daddy, Mama, my sister June, and I stepped out the front door into a world of white magic.

The road was unpaved then and there was a good eight inches of snow already there and more falling. Daddy, who always loved an adventure, would turn the flashlight beam back the way we'd come to show me and June how fast our tracks were filling. I had the strangest feeling looking back at those four sets of tracks disappearing around the curve. It seemed we were the only people alive, just us four. But oh, we had set out on the most delicious of adventures!

We saw the unnatural glow of the broken power line even before we rounded the curve. We could hear a pop-ping and cracking sound and could smell a strange smell, like metal burning. Daddy had all of us wait while he dis-appeared around the curve. I got as close to the edge of the road as I could trying to peep around it. All I could see was that strange blue-white light. Then I saw Daddy's black shadow shape coming back, the light behind him making him look like a haint.

"Daddy, is that you?" I asked when he'd gotten close enough to where I thought he'd be able to hear me.

No answer.

"Daddy!" I said again, fear making my voice rise.

No answer, but I heard it growl.

I broke to run back toward Mama, squealing (even though I was pretty sure it had to be Daddy. This was, after all, a magic night, and we were on an adventure, where anything could happen).

All of a sudden my feet left the ground, and I was sud-denly up in the familiar arms of my Daddy.

"I'll save you, Sealy. I won't let it git you!"

Daddy nuzzled my neck with his whisker-stubbled cheek, and I shrieked with laughter.

"Ervin, you stop that. She's making enough racket to wake all of Sodom. Let's get on to Flossie's. I'm freezing to death," Mama said.

"We'll need to go the old road 'cause the power line's down across the road just beyond the curve. It's burnin' and doin' a little snake dance halfway across the road," Daddy said.

The old road was the road down by the graveyard, the same road where my Uncle Herb had met the strange thing that had broken up the infamous poker game.

"Well, let's get on then," Mama said.

We turned and walked back up to the old Miss Fedrick's House, the only house in Sodom that us young'uns knew for certain was haunted.

Daddy was laughing and talking, waving his flashlight around, but I was quiet. And, so was June. Daddy's light would careen around and accidentally hit one of the windows in the old house. Once, I could just about swear I saw something flit by a window.

Then Daddy got real quiet and started acting real nervous. Finally, he stopped dead still and shined the flashlight's beam up the path leading to the graveyard.

"What was that?" he whispered.

"Now you stop it, Ervin. You're scaring the young'uns." Mama herself shot a nervous glance toward the path.

Daddy's laughter broke up the night. "Just the young'uns? You sure it's just the young'uns I'm a makin' nervous?"

We got to Flossie's and stomped the snow off on the porch. Daddy knocked and hollered until his cousin Hester's sleepy face appeared at the door.

"Wake up, Hester, and let us in. It's come the biggest snow you'll ever see, and it's broke a power line."

Hester opened the door. It's hard to describe the kind of warmth we entered there in my great-aunt Flossie's old log house. Oh, there was the woodstove's heat that made my cheeks and hands tingle. But there was more. It was a welcoming warmth that I have come to identify so much with those early years in Sodom. The warmth of close family, the warmth of close affection, the warmth of familiarity, the warmth of love. The house smelled of supper and sleep. It was a good smell.

The grown-ups talked for a while about the weather. Hank, my cousin, and I checked each other out in this new light. We'd never seen each other this late at night. His hair stuck out in stiff dabs all over his head, and his eyes had sleep in them.

"You look funny," Hank grinned at me.

"You do too," I replied.

Soon we were playing and laughing, just like always.

Aunt Flossie fried up some bacon from the hog she'd killed back in the fall. Mama and Hester made gravy and biscuits, and June was sent down in the root cellar after homemade "fruit" and jelly.

We ate breakfast by the glow of kerosene lamps. I have never eaten food that tasted as good as that breakfast.

Daddy retold the story about Hester's brother Wesley and the crawdad.

Wesley was my aunt Flossie's and uncle Herb's next-to-the-oldest child. He was always pulling pranks and cutting up. One morning Aunt Flossie sent Wesley to the spring to carry in a bucket of water. While he was down at the spring house, Wesley noticed a big crayfish in the clear stream. He picked it up and put it over in the water bucket and never said a word about it. He figured to startle Aunt Flossie.

The gravy made up too thick that morning, so Flossie reached in and got a dipper of water to thin it out. The biscuits were already done, so she dumped the water in without looking, got the bread out, and brought everything to the table. They commenced to eating.

Midway through the meal, Herb says, "Sakes, this is good gravy Floss. What kind of meat did you put in it? Tastes right peculiar, but it's good."

"Didn't add no meat this mornin'. All I put in it was a

dipper of water from the bucket Wesley fetched from the spring."

All eyes went to Wesley. Wesley grinned and said, "Crawdad gravy, Pap – just crawdad gravy."

Herb made a little ek-k-k sound and clapped both hands over his mouth and bolted for the kitchen door.

Daddy and Flossie laughed, remembering. Me and Hank were starting to nod over our empty plates by this time, so Hester and Mama led us upstairs.

At the top of the stairs was a small area separated from the steps by a wooden stair rail. I suppose it must've been designed as an upstairs parlor, but Aunt Flossie had put two little beds there. Mama bedded me in one, and Hester put Hank in the other.

After Hester and Mama went back down the stairs, we lay there in the dark talking young'un talk. We decided to ride his sled tomorrow, build an igloo, and walk up to the Indian Graveyard to see what it would look like in the snow. When Hank finally stopped talking, I lay there for a while longer looking out the window at the bare branches of the apple tree. The grown-ups were talking softly down in the kitchen. I heard Daddy laugh and Mama shush him.

And I remember thinking, oh, I want to always remember this. Oh, I hope I will always remember this . . .

Afterword

. . . .

This place called Sodom exists only in my memory. The name has even been changed. The people I write about have, for the most part, retired to the graveyards that dot the hillsides there in my childhood home. The roads have been paved, the mobile homes have altered the views, telephones ring in every house, and most of the young folks who still live there leave bright and early for jobs in Greeneville, Tennessee, or Asheville, North Carolina. Sodom did not escape the dance to the tune called "Progress."

Granny's house still sits up at the end of the Burton Cove. Her grandson lives in it now. Breaddaddy and Ma's house sits empty most of the time, except during family reunions . . . then the walls of the old homeplace absorb the sounds of several generations of Nortons, Adams, and Wallins. And more: The cousins have married and brought in new blood. Unfamiliar maiden names and last names are now linked with the familiar. New facial features have begun to emerge.

This past June I sat, banjo held loosely in my lap, and looked at the crowd of aunts, uncles, cousins, and spouses. I had to smile as I studied each face. What would Breaddaddy have thought? What would the old man have thought? The same old man who asked my father to stop the car on the top of Lonesome Mountain as they were returning from a trip to Philadelphia. He got out of the car, went to his knees, leaned over and kissed the ground and said, "God bless old Sodom!"

The children played and chased each other through what used to be a pasture there off the back porch. The old outhouse is covered in poison ivy vines. The spring house was torn down a few years ago. The kids were told sharply not to play in the old barn. Snakes, their parents warned.

The uncles and aunts, now well into their sixties, seventies, and even early eighties, sit in the shade talking. My gaze rests on my mother's face. She sits staring dreamily up at what Breadddaddy called the upper fields, grown up in trees now. What must she be seeing? All of a sudden she turns her head slightly, and her soft brown eyes connect with mine. She smiles. I stand and walk to her and kneel next to her chair. Wisps of her silky red hair have escaped the hairpins and blow in the early summer breeze.

"It's all changed," she says. She absently reaches up and smoothes her hair back away from her face. I am struck by the fragile look of her hand . . . the thin skin, shot through with blue veins, dotted with what Granny called age spots, the slender fingers bent and twisted by arthritis. Suddenly a memory of Ma smoothing her hair and tucking it back into the ever-present bun washes over me. Then it's gone.

Mama turns slightly in her chair and she looks to the corner of the house where one of the kids is inspecting Ma's lilac bush. "Mama used to say it somehow made washing dishes easier if you had a headfull of lilac."

I nod, I've heard that before.

"I was thinking about the old Willis Norton house. Do you remember it? It used to sit across the branch back down the road a ways. Poppy said they formed a human man-chain from the saw mill over on Big Laurel all the way to the Burton Cove. They moved every single piece of lumber to build that house just that way."

"I remember the house. Mary and A.B. lived in it when I was little," I answer.

Mama talks about her childhood for a while and then I'm summoned to the front porch. Appears one of my boys has need of me. And as I walk around the house I turn and look back at her. She sits, dreaming her dreams of childhood and young womanhood.

That's another story, my mind whispers.

Acknowledgments

. . . .

I would like to thank the following people for helping to make this book a reality:

Dellie (Granny) Chandler Norton, Bob (Breaddaddy) and Emily (Ma) Norton, Inez Chandler, Vergie and Cas Wallin, Berzilla Wallin, Uncle Byard Ray, Granny Cloe Stanton and Pap Neil Adams, Fannie Adams Leake, and all the other family and kin who shaped me into the person I am.

Bobby McMillon, my dear, faithful friend who shares my memories and makes me feel not quite so alone.

Lee Smith, my friend and trusted mentor, this book would never have happened had it not been for you, and that's a fact.

David Perry, my friend and editor, for all those dark times of self-doubt in which you carried me with your belief in me as a writer.

Sarah Nawrocki and all the other fine folks at the UNC Press for all the hard work and hours y'all put into this book.

Jerry Adams, my cousin, for all those conversations and stories.

June Adams Gahagan, for loving me unconditionally all these years.

Cathy Stone, for her encouragement, support, and all those seemingly endless hours proofing the first draft and the second draft and the third draft and on and on and on.

Allen Stines, for all those many hours typing the first draft of this book.

Taylor Barnhill, for your suggestions and advice.

CeCe Conway, for your interest and support of this project.

Robbie Gaulding, Marilyn McMinn McCredie, Toot Evett, Lena Jean Ray, Janet Adams Crowe, Aunt Robena Adams, Uncle Wayne Adams, Keith Ray, Sharon Ray, Myrtle Leake Ray, Jane Goforth, Sue Vilcinskas, Ronnie Ramsey, Laura Boosinger, Chris Worley, Maggie Lauterer, Connie Regan-Blake, Barbara Freeman, Barbara Lau, Phillip and Jane Rhodes, Reg and Micki Ledoux, Jill Wilson, Jeri Board, Judy Boyer, Mary Wynn Beaman, Kay Byer, Doris Davenport, Chris Comer, Cherie Sheppard, Jim Wayne Miller,

Wayne Martin, and all those other numerous folks who make up my "family" of friends that have listened to me, given advice, and supported me through it all.

Vicki Skemp, for doing the final proofing of the book.

Jim Taylor, my husband, for the endless ear and the love and encouragement given in big, daily doses, and for the light at the end of my first forty years.

Melanie Rice and Hart and Andrew Barnhill, my young'uns, for teaching me patience, devotion, and what this word love is all about.

Ervin and Neple Adams, my parents, for the genes, the acceptance and fierce loyalty, and all the memories you gave me from your past and those you lived through with me.

And a kind, loving, and forgiving God for the talents He gave me.